ENDORSEMENTS

"This is the account of an amazing journey that connected two people from opposite sides of the globe. As I read the story, my heart kept saying, 'Only God!' Only God could have orchestrated such an adventure. Kristi and Lukas' story will embolden you to listen to children all around you and to listen for God's leading in your own life as well."

~Dr. Doug Kyle, Pastor,
Green Valley Church, San Diego, CA

"Kristi Wilkinson takes us to Romania, but it is her adopted son, Lukas, that takes us Home. Only Jesus could write a story as beautiful as this one."

~Tommy Spaulding, *New York Times* Bestselling Author,
The Heart-Led Leader and *It's Not Just Who You Know*

"Engaging, compelling, and heart-wrenching."

~Jim Brogan, former NBA player for the San Diego Clippers,
Author, Speaker, and Mentor for Athletes in the NBA, NFL, and MLB

"A thoroughly engaging read. Heartbreaking, yet heartwarming, and inspirational at the same time."

~Dr. Jack Gyves, Former Superintendent of Schools
Petaluma, CA, School District

THE CHILD WHO LISTENS

ONE WOMAN, ONE BOY, AND THE MIRACLES THAT BROUGHT THEM TOGETHER

Kristi Wilkinson

AN AUTHORSOURCE IMPRINT

Published by Third Day Press
An Imprint of AuthorSource, Inc.
www.authorsourcemedia.com

Cover Design by Sharon Okamoto
Interior Layout Design by AuthorSource, Inc.

ISBN: 978-1-947939-75-2
E-book ISBN: 978-1-947939-76-9
Library of Congress: 2018914400

Printed in the United States

CONTENTS

*Proceeds from this book will be given
to support orphans around the globe.*

ACKNOWLEDGMENTS

There are many people that helped to make this book a reality. Firstly, I thank Lukas for insisting at age nine that I write this book. I want to thank those who encouraged me along the way, including my mom, Sandi, Doug Kyle, Peggy Noe, Pam Silberman, and Stephanie Cain who, for over seventeen years, encouraged me to complete the project. A few co-workers, including Jazmin Herrera and Jose Lopez, asked me weekly for over a year how the book was coming along, and urged me to keep writing. I am grateful for my husband, Tim Flowers, for reading the book in its infancy and giving me an idea for a much-needed stylistic change. His patience allowed for the writing time I had to block into my schedule. He also spent hours helping me to convert my slide-film photos into digital media so that they could be seen by readers. My dad, Jim Wilkinson, also cheered me on from the sidelines to finish this project.

As for the editing process, first, I am truly indebted to Carolyn Hinkley, since she painstakingly delved through and edited the entire document word by word, and came to the end and said, "You returned to Romania with Lukas and gave me three pages. I need more! Give me more details and I will re-edit the entire book again." And she did this as a complete stranger who felt called to help me with this project.

I thank Chris Wise for helping me to convert my book from one computer to another. Christina Hammerberg was very helpful in giving me some wonderful writing tips after reading the first thirty pages. I thank Lindsay Nestor who suggested some writing ideas, and also gave feedback on which of Lukas' quotes to include.

One friend, Chrissy Stone, deserves repeated thanks for taking time on Thanksgiving day to help me bind the original manuscript so that I could send it to the editor. She also created and launched my facebook page for the book to invite friends into my dream. I thank Carol Groseth for editing and giving insight on the first few chapters of the book. I am grateful for Megan Shutes who spent hours editing the last section of the book with helpful ideas.

I thank my cousin, Todd Hawkins, who also went through the front half of the book with incredible detail because he wanted it to be the best that it could be. His daughter Sophia Hawkins also caught a few errors! I thank John and Marie Graber for giving editing advice and moral support, and suggesting not to "over-edit" the book.

I thank my mom, Sandi Wilkinson, for sitting next to me at the computer, hour after hour late into the night, listening to certain sections for their clarity and also for reminding me of certain stories that I had not included. She helped to edit, keep the grammar clean, and helped with my flow of thought—I couldn't have completed this the way I did without her. Iorela Karlsson was mostly responsible for ensuring that the historical facts surrounding Casa Alba and its inception were accurate. She read the book and gave over forty corrections, sent from Sweden on her iPhone!

I thank Sharon Okamoto, my lifelong friend, for having the creative ideas for my book cover and for the incredible job she did in designing the cover. She continued to give graphic input for the interior of the book. A co-worker, Ricky Marcic, was also instrumental in getting my facebook page noticed, as I was not too skilled with the internet or social media. Mahri Aste was also helpful in spreading the word about my book on facebook.

I thank Dawn Golding for scanning and downloading my photos so that they were accessible on the computer. I thank Jessica Yackley for digitally assisting me with the photos so that I could write inscriptions below them. Jerome Stewart and Erica Viviani also assisted with the photos and made sure that the last few pictures made it to print.

I thank my nephew Damiano for intently listening to Lukas' thoughts and insisting that others hear of them. I thank my sister Julie Peccedi and my niece Tatiana for helping me with photo selection and graphic ideas for the book. I thank Bruce Barbour for his time and encouragement to publish this book and for giving input about the printing process.

Before I was aware that an author photo was necessary, Cindy Kyle offered to take my photograph for the cover. She, and her assistant, Ryleigh DeJong, did an amazing job and I can't thank them enough for their time and efforts. I thank Rocky Cheng for his willingness to read the book and recommend an endorsement from Tommy Spalding. I thank Jim Brogan and Dr. Jack Gyves for taking the time to read and endorse my book. Many of my co-workers at Casa de las Campanas deserve thanks, especially Lauren Dunker and Emily Vaught, for assisting me with downloads and techniques so that I could edit the publisher's initial book interior. Thank you to Noah Lottig, who created the beautiful book trailer video for *A Child Who Listens*, available at https://bit.ly/2R34f1g.

Lastly, and most importantly, I must thank Beth Lottig for being my friend, "book coach" and mentor, and for believing in this book before I knew it was meant for more than a few friends and family. I thank her for coaching me, and for letting me know which step to complete next, from the cover page, to a Facebook page to help announce the book, to endorsements, to a book proposal, and then finally to work together to publish this book. I feel she was supposed to be involved with this from the beginning. I am humbled that Beth spent more than three years during the exhaustive steps of this process before she knew she would help with its publishing. It has been an incredible experience to walk to the finish line with her by my side. I truly thank her with every fiber in my being, for sharing my joy and excitement in this labor of love. It would not be what it is without her dedication and belief that my story was supposed to be heard.

Since I was quite the novice with computer skills, I once again thank my son Lukas for the countless hours he assisted me with learning everything I needed to know so I could write this book on something other than paper. He assisted in sending it to over ten people and when it would occasionally fail to send, he would repeat this process in a different way. When I would ask him for help "one more time"—although I know it became a chore—he would help me anyway. Without him, this book wouldn't "be"!

Finally, I thank God for the chance to adopt and be a mother to my son, Lukas, and for leading and directing my steps in writing this book.

PART 1

REFLECTION

He stood beside me and gently tapped my shoulder, hesitant to wake me, but afraid not to. This was his routine every night at about two in the morning. This night, he posed a question that haunts me to this day, "De che, Kitty, de che?" asked in his native Romanian tongue. I understood this question to be, "Why, Kristi, why?" In his language he continued to ask, "Why do the children at Casa Alba walk alone in life without mamas and papas? Why?" Casa Alba, an orphanage in the northwestern region of Transylvania, was the only home that four-year-old Lukas had ever known.

How would I answer this question? I could barely open my eyes, and felt like I was half-way between a dream and reality. It would be hard to answer such a question in the middle of the day, let alone at two in the morning. Gently whispering, I said, "I don't know, Lukas, I don't know. I wish every child had someone to call mama or papa." I wish I could have given him a better answer. I wish I could have assured him that no child would ever have to walk alone.

Lifting him up, I carried him back to his room, placing his light blue blanket over his small frame. I knelt beside him and continued to stroke his forehead, singing "Amazing Grace." I had to keep singing until he fell asleep or his fear would keep him awake. He was afraid I would leave and he would be left alone—afraid since he was no longer near his roommates Gusztav, Darius and Laurentiu, whom he had known as brothers at Casa Alba. I continued to sing. Fifteen songs were hummed before he stopped opening his eyes to make sure that I was still beside him. My voice was becoming hoarse, and I was so delirious that I started to create songs to the tune of "Silent Night," a song that was calming to him. His breathing started to deepen and I knew it was safe to inch my way out of the room and back to the couch, so I could get some rest. I closed my eyes, but sleep escaped me. I couldn't get his question out of my mind:"De Che, de che? Why? Why do they walk alone?"

CHAPTER 1

My Dream

I have a story to tell. A true story of a child named, Lukas, who I met in 1997, more than nineteen years ago, and who later became my son. I work with the elderly, and have shared this story with those lying in hospital beds who had ears to listen. Time and time again, they would say to me, "You have to write a book. I want to hear everything that happened." Shortly after I adopted my son, my pastor, Doug Kyle, asked me to share part of my journey on a Sunday morning during church. As I sat in his office, sharing a few details before the service, I told him that I felt I should write the story. But something kept holding me back. He simply said to me, "Maybe the story isn't finished." Little did I know that it had only begun.

Several years later, when my son was eleven, he said to me, "It is time." I said, "Time for what?" He said, "Time to write the book—what God has spoken to the child. There is a war on faith, and God wants people to know who He is." I had never mentioned "the book" to him before. This was confirmation that it was time to start writing.

I had kept a journal of all of the things that Lukas said when he was younger. I wrote things in this journal partly because other moms suggested that I catch those childlike sayings before forgetting them, and partly because the things he said to me seemed out of the ordinary for a child, and I thought I needed to record them. I didn't have the experience as a mom to know what was ordinary for a child to say. Those journal entries have been woven throughout this story to share the miracle of his adoption. In a sense, it is as though his thoughts were hand-stitched to produce the story in its entirety—one that I never could have imagined.

CHAPTER 2

THE YEARNING TO SERVE

When I was about twenty-one years old, and a senior in college, I felt torn. The aspiration of becoming a physical therapist had been planted in me in ninth grade after watching a little boy struggle to walk in a set of parallel bars. I felt a calling inside me to something beyond books and memorizing lots of facts to get the grade. I said to God—as if somehow I could persuade him to alter His plans—"If you want me to get into Physical Therapy (PT) school, then let that happen and I will go. But if you want me to join the Peace Corps, please open that door instead."

A secret place inside me wanted to open the door myself to some distant land. My mom, Sandi, had encouraged me throughout my life to serve others. And I was truly exhausted from the intensity of college. Friends questioned why I had isolated myself at times while in college, and had hidden in the science library until midnight rather than socializing as much as they did. But I had a dream . . . and I felt this dream had to be realized.

I tried to ensure that my path would lead to the Peace Corps by applying to only two PT schools, knowing that most students with the same goal were applying to five to ten schools due to the competitive nature of the field. Although I longed for a break from the books, I also knew that if I were accepted into PT school, I could perhaps use those skills in some place of need. I shared that secret desire with my roommates from the University of Richmond, Tory Robinson, Scottie Hill, and Sandi Dollar, and they encouraged me to follow it no matter where it took me. Some other country was calling me, I just had no idea which one it was.

As I opened the envelope from Hahnemann University, I anxiously hesitated and sat holding the letter in my hands for a moment. The first Pennsylvania therapy program had already given me a rejection letter, and I was truly relieved. There was a fifty-fifty chance that I would be packing my bags and traveling abroad. I was ready to go feed the hungry, but when I opened the envelope, I learned of another fate: inner-city Philadelphia, where Hahnemann University was located, would become my next home. Two more years would be dedicated to "the books." Hopefully I could learn what it would take for me to travel across the seas to help those in need.

PT school was challenging, even grueling at times. I began school in July of 1989, two months after I finished college in Virginia. I was in class with sixty other eager students from 8:00 a.m. to 4:00 p.m. I allowed myself one hour to eat and exercise, then studied from 6:00 p.m. until midnight. On weekends, I studied from sun-up until way beyond sun-down. At one point, I became so overwhelmed with the distinct odor of the cadaver lab and the pathways of neuroanatomy that I thought I would just give up. The stress eventually weighed so heavily on me that I made an appointment with a professor named Phil McClure to discuss the possibility of dropping-out. After our meeting, Dr. McClure wrote something to me that I will never forget. He said, "You have been called—called for a purpose. That purpose is to become a PT." I would post the yellow sticky note bearing these words in a journal I kept by my bedside, and for many years they served as a source of comfort and peace in times of uncertainty.

After finishing PT school in Philadelphia, my mom and I drove across the country to my parents' home in Southern California to prepare for the board exams, while deciding where in the world I wanted to work. I had taken this same road trip the year before with my friend from PT school, Susie Otero Lefebvre, when my parents moved to San Diego from the East Coast. During our cross-country trek, we both fell in love with Colorado, and Susie quickly decided that Boulder would be her next home. While passing through the Rocky Mountain State, I tore a page from the Yellow

Pages that listed hospitals near Denver (such was life before Google!). While staying with my parents, I called several Denver-based hospitals. When I learned that ten out of ten hospitals needed physical therapists, the decision was easy—Denver was where I would begin my career.

CHAPTER 3

THE DOOR OPENS IN DENVER

My first job as a physical therapist was at Mercy Medical Center in 1991. An idea blossomed that I should get some medical experience at Mercy, then form a team of doctors and travel overseas right away. I met the hospital chaplain, Father Gold, and I shared my dream with him. He had the same dream to form a team to help those in need. I thought that this was confirmation of my future plans. But just where were we supposed to go? Although I prayed and prayed for direction, I didn't hear the answer.

Three years after I shared that dream with Father Gold, I came home to my apartment after work on a late summer day and saw my roommate's *Denver Post* lying on my kitchen table. Worthy of mention is that I had come days away from buying and moving into a small house in Washington Park, alone, where I wouldn't have had a newspaper. I rarely read the paper since I couldn't seem to find the time. I volunteered with teenagers in a youth group at my church, and their issues weighed heavier on my heart than the national debt or who was running in the Senate race.

My roommate, Beth McElroy—also a PT from Philadelphia—read the paper and kept me informed of world and local events. But that day, I happened to pick up the newspaper, and the photo I saw on the front page would change my life forever. It was chilling. In it were rows and rows of baby cribs, laid out in a diagonal pattern with muted colors that masked the faces of the children inside. A seemingly countless number of institutional white metal cribs stared back at me. The image first appealed to my love of photography, yet when I read the article attached to the photo, a wave of compassion was provoked in me.

Those metal bars held children like prisoners when mothers' and fathers' hands could not. I read the article below, and it mentioned that these children were orphans from Romania. There were thousands of abandoned children, and the country needed help. The babies in the photo were victims of Nicolae Ceausescu, the dictator of Romania, who had taken the children captive in an attempt to build an army of orphans. His twisted dream was that this army would then make Romania a superpower. His attempt had failed, he and his wife had been executed, and thousands of children were warehoused far from their parents who didn't have the funds to support them.

November 16, 2003—Age 7

Lukas was asking me about war and he said, "Sometimes we're stronger than bad kings. When God sees a bad king, he makes us stronger to come against them."

The article revealed that the children needed nurturing arms to hold and rock them, as there were not enough caregivers for each child. It also explained that the kids were delayed developmentally due to lack of movement and touch. In PT school, I had treated children with similar delays on a pediatric internship. The photograph, and the plight of these neglected children, captivated me. At that moment, I knew that I would go to Romania. Finally, I had discovered that mysterious "somewhere" that had eluded me for years.

I told Beth—who shares my passion for photography and love of children—about the photograph and how it had spoken to me and she encouraged me to follow my heart. When I look back on how close I came to buying that house and moving out, my heart skips a beat. I'm so grateful for the voice inside that told me to stay in that apartment with Beth on Humboldt Street. That decision to stay, the gripping photo: These seemingly insignificant slices of everyday life would guide me along a path that I could not have anticipated. I am forever grateful to Beth for standing beside me as this improbable journey progressed.

CHAPTER 4

THE UNCERTAIN ROAD TO ROMANIA

I called a friend named Pat to tell her about the photograph of the orphans and how it had spoken to me. A former PT at Mercy Medical Center, Pat had retired in her sixties and was someone I admired for her inspirational faith. Since she was a mentor to me, I asked her to help me find my way to Romania. Months passed, and one day I was paged at the nurse's station on the orthopedic floor. She had worked on that floor, so they let her call go through to me. She had heard that a group called " Operation Blessing" would be traveling to Romania to work with an orphanage. I could barely contain my excitement. I called a toll-free number from the nurses' station and requested that the Virginia-based organization send me an application. Their team was to leave in a month, and I was already mentally packing my bags. The door to this daydream abruptly slammed shut when a staff member contacted me and asked if I had a passport. Having never traveled outside the U.S., I had no passport, and when I told her this, she kindly informed me that there would be no way of processing the passport in time for the trip that November of 1994. To say I was devastated would be an understatement. I wondered whether my vision would become a reality.

As the Spring of 1995 arrived, my dream seemed to fade away. Mercy Hospital announced that it was closing its doors, and would leave 800 of us without jobs. This was disturbing news, but finding a job wasn't my biggest concern. I was more concerned with never making it overseas. I decided to fill out the volunteer application anyway and get my passport

THE CHILD WHO LISTENS

processed so that I would be prepared if another opportunity surfaced to go to Romania.

In fact, the job search was very brief. While I was documenting my daily treatment notes at the nurse's station at Mercy, a co-worker informed me of an opportunity. A temporary job as a PT at a nursing home had become available, and within a week after Mercy closed, I took the place of a therapist on maternity leave. During this time, I received a letter informing me that I had been accepted to travel with Operation Blessing. I was disappointed to notice that they were not returning to Romania, but would be traveling instead to Kazakhstan. Furthermore, I wasn't sure that my schedule would permit the trip since I would be required to commit three months to the temporary job assignment. I would also need to come up with $2,500 to cover all of the travel and living costs. I thought, *How can I raise that money and travel, only to return unemployed*?

Operation Blessing informed me that the trip was to leave on September 6. I looked at the terms of the agreement to fill the maternity leave, and found that my job at the nursing facility would end September 5. This was the answer I had prayed for. The timing was more than perfect. I didn't feel the need to worry about raising the money or finding a job when I came home. God would take care of that. This door had opened. Excited for the adventure, I committed to go.

The next day at work, I was paged to the nurse's station at the nursing home—Operation Blessing was on the line. They called me to ask if I had more time in my schedule as they were adding two weeks in China to the trip. I figured, "I'll be without a job anyway, so what's two more weeks?"

I wrote letters to friends and family and got an overwhelming response. My friends from college were the first to get in touch with me. When I opened the first two letters, from Scottie Hill Belfi, and Mahri Aste, I was so thankful for the notes of support. These two and other friends not only encouraged me to take my first trip, they graciously gave donations that made the trip to China and Kazakhstan possible. I remember the tears streaming down my cheeks as I looked at the letters, humbled that my friends would help to fulfill this dream. With the help of friends and family members, I was able to raise the funds needed for the trip and soon I was packing my bags.

13

CHAPTER 5

JOURNEY WITH OPERATION BLESSING

September 1995 marked my first journey outside the U.S., six years after I felt the call to serve. My experiences in Kazakhstan and China had an enormous impact on my life. In Kazakhstan, I worked with a group of people called Uyghurs, who were considered outcasts in that society. Our team hoped that we could be a blessing to them, as we could see that they lived in a state of poverty, and we suspected that they had little to no access to medical care. We lived in a building in close proximity to where the local trash was burned. Every evening, at about the same time, the acrid burning smell would waft through the windows and seemingly permeate every fiber of my clothing. But as our team held our medical clinics and walked through the disheveled neighborhoods where the residents resided, I found that this disparaged minority lived among heaps of trash, with raw sewage running down the streets between their meager homes. Although I dreaded the evening hours that came with the smell of burning trash—hours in which my lungs felt tight, and my breath too short—the aroma could be seen as sweet when compared to what the the locals had to bear.

September 2002—Age 6

I was getting ready to go a funeral for a fourteen-year-old named Katie. She was the niece of my friend Susie LeFebvre, and I was overwhelmed with sadness for the family's loss of such a young child. I told Lukas that she had just passed away, and he asked me why I was so sad. He then asked me, "Does she get to run in the clouds and sing with the angels now?" I asked him to talk about this a little bit more. He explained that he knew that she would get to do these things. He was just asking me when she would get this chance. His picture of Katie helped to ease my sadness. I hoped it would do the same for her family.

CHAPTER 6

FROM A CURSE TO A BLESSING

After we finished teaching basic health to mostly women and children, we traveled to a small village where most people gawked when they saw me. They had never seen anyone with blonde hair, let alone an American. My memory of the village was of dust and dry heat, and of people with sun-scorched skin—their wrinkles as deep as the burdens they carried.

One particular image burned into my memory of a woman who brought her toddler to me as he couldn't yet walk. I wondered why she held the child at a distance, as if at any moment he could have dropped from her arms. Through an interpreter, I learned that their culture taught that her child was evil because of his deformities, and that she had brought this evil upon him. I asked God to help me speak to this mother about her child with a spirit of love. With one look, I could tell that the child had Down Syndrome. Because my mom had taught a Sunday school class for children with Down Syndrome in Philadelphia for fifteen years, I was very comfortable talking with the woman about her child. I asked her if I could hold him, and she seemed shocked. I learned that no one else had ever held him, lest the evil be spread to them. Through the interpreter, I told her that I believed each child was a gift from God and that her child was as special as any other child. I explained that he could grow up to bless her in ways that she could not yet understand. I watched her as the translator tried to explain this to her, and I watched one of the most beautiful things transpire before me. Her face, which before had worn a heavy and

16

withdrawn expression, now had a lightness that radiated from her eyes so intensely that I could almost feel the heat on my hands as I held her son. After I handed her son back to her, she held him with such joy—perhaps for the first time. If I left that country and its people without doing one more thing, I felt, perhaps, I had made a difference for this mother and child, and had experienced one of the richest moments of my life.

CHAPTER 7

HEALING WOUNDS

We held a clinic in Alma Ata, one of the biggest cities in Kazakhstan, and saw patients for eight hours each day. The first day, I met one man who was pouring salt into his wound for weeks in the hope that it would heal. Similar to a saline rinse, his method was effective at cleaning the wound, but was not the best way to heal it, as it would leave the wound dessicated, and such dryness would prevent healing. I was able to apply a moist dressing that would promote the healing of the wound, and I wished him well.

When I noticed that the man had returned on the last day of the clinic, I confess to some worry, concerned that perhaps our Western ways were not working as well as I had expected. He came to me and showed me his wound. Although he couldn't speak English, he gave me a big hug and beamed from ear to ear, saying that it already showed improvement. Those days at Mercy Medical Center performing wound care—and learning that wet-to-dry dressings were a thing of the past—had come in handy that day for that man. Again, the feeling was so rewarding, and I just hoped that I could continue to help the poor and infirm in China as well.

CHAPTER 8

RIVERBED HIGHWAY

We left Kazakhstan, where soldiers in khaki outfits with rifles to match lined the airport, and flew into the Western region of China to a "small" city that turned out to be quite large by my standards. I arrived in Urumqi to find that it was bustling with two million people, all of whom seemed to be on bicycles. A bit weary from the travel, I immediately noticed that not one person was overweight, let alone chubby. Perhaps if we Americans just rode our bicycles to work or to a friend's house more often, we might not need Jenny Craig's packaged frozen meals, or grapefruit diets and juice cleanses.

Our next venture was to travel from Urumqi to a small town named Korla, in the Western region. We traveled in a van that took ten of us through countryside that resembled the painted desert in Arizona. The trip began smoothly, but I sensed an adventure beginning as the asphalt road came to an abrupt end. The van had veered off the road onto the only available path—a dried-up river bed, littered with boulders as big as bass drums. We would remain on this makeshift road for the next ten hours, traveling through the night. A woman on our team named Lori Cordes sat beside me, and as we were jostled back and forth, both of us began to get giddy. We had just wondered aloud if we would be able to get any sleep on this roller coaster ride when the van hit a boulder and tipped onto two wheels, then sprung back to an upright position, flipping us upwards, bouncing both of our heads off the ceiling of the van. We exchanged one glance and burst into hysterical laughter at the thought of trying to sleep.

The next day, after that sleepless night, our team met with a group of doctors for lunch. I was famished, and since I enjoyed eating in Chinatown in Philadelphia, I was eager for the meal to arrive. The large platters looked lovely until I gazed at what was on them: fish heads, duck feet, and mutton. Where was the white rice? I quickly learned I couldn't ask for any or I would insult someone. People only asked for white rice if they weren't satisfied with the meal. I took one bite of the fat-laced mutton and knew it would be my last taste. Hoping that no one would notice, I snuck the mutton from my plate and acted as if I dropped something on the floor so that I could slip the piece of mutton into my shoe. I did this repeatedly, also using my sock as a hiding place for the pieces of fish that I couldn't ingest. Finally the lunch came to an end. I managed to escape the meal undiscovered—only my empty stomach was aware.

We visited a hospital later that day. Our team was to discuss infection control. I noticed that no one used gloves while working, and that patients were carried on stretchers rather than being rolled on them. It was evident that hazmat suits would not be available in this hospital. The halls had a damp, musty smell, as if the mildew were dripping from the ceiling as we walked from room to room. Although we were in a hospital where the goal was recovery, the air was so ladened with affliction I couldn't imagine anyone healing. I also noticed that patient's family members were the nurse assistants at this hospital and that there was no kitchen. Families had to bring food to their ailing loved ones. I thought of all of the Americans who grumbled when a turkey sandwich or chicken cacciatore didn't please them at the hospital—they might think twice about whining to the nutritionists or kitchen staff after seeing conditions in this part of the world.

I woke up the morning we were to fly to Beijing and I noticed an ache and a rumbling in my stomach that was becoming ever more uncomfortable. Now I know I cannot compare my experience to those on the show Survivor who had to search and scramble through the rainforest for scraps of food, but I was hungry—really hungry. Obviously, I missed the memo that all of the other seasoned workers on my team received, informing us that we should bring snacks on this trip—and lots of them. One of the physicians on my team who was a veteran volunteer on overseas trips had an entire jar of peanut butter, trail mix, M&M's, and protein bars among other treats. Me, I had nada—nothing. I didn't want to appear selfish or dependent so I didn't ask any of the other team members for any of their wonderful items from their stash.

Desperate for food, and optimistic about what breakfast might bring, I imagined some type of filling meal, perhaps with a porridge-like consistency. I will never forget walking into a dimly lit room and sitting at a small round table with a simple red table cloth. My mouth started to water as a staff member approached our table. Though I expected him to ask what I wanted for breakfast, he instead informed us that our meals would be brought soon. Minutes later, a small empty cup was placed next to me that might have held a few ounces of liquid, and warm tea was poured inside. Water was apparently not a part of the morning routine. Next, a small bowl, only twice the size of the tea cup, was placed in front of me and I peered inside. It was filled with an opaque grey-white liquid and had a few rice pellets floating inside. Since it was like a broth but with no true substance, I looked for a spoon, hoping that I could at least enjoy the hydration. To my dismay, only chopsticks accompanied the napkins on the table. I had tried often to master the use of chopsticks during this trip, as they were the only utensils available, but I was still a novice. I couldn't imagine trying to get a grasp of one of the pellets of rice with the chopsticks, but I gave it my best effort. I felt as though I were trying to catch a minnow in a fishbowl with tweezers—it was close to impossible. I glanced around the room to see if anyone was just picking up the small bowls and drinking the fluid inside, but I noticed that the locals were eating the soup with chopsticks.

Lady luck was not on my side. I fished around in the bowl with the chopsticks to no avail, as the five pieces of rice escaped the big catch every time. After a dozen attempts, I surrendered, somewhat like the defeated man in *The Old Man and the Sea*, after the fish he had followed for days evaded him. Frustrated, I leaned back in my chair, with the ever-present symphony of sounds from my abdomen now audible to others at my table. I hoped that Beijing would bring an end to my fast and to the gnawing ache in my stomach.

Shortly after landing in Beijing, we learned that our plans to work in a small village had been thwarted when the village leader unexpectedly died. Our team leader told us he needed to split our team into several groups and he would choose our work destination. He said,"Kristi, since you are the only physical therapist, I want you to go to an orphanage near Changchung." I could hardly believe it. I never mentioned my vision of going to an orphanage with anyone on the team, so I was thrilled with his choice. I thought, *Maybe this is it. Maybe I am not meant to go to Romania. Maybe this orphanage in China is the one meant for me.*

With great anticipation, I boarded a train bound for Changchung, in the Eastern region of China, with four others from our team. I was one of the first to board, so I found it easy to slip into my seat. No sooner had I sat down, however, when in flooded many other passengers. A few people sat in my row. Feeling outnumbered, I decided to switch seats to join another team member. As I got up, I was pushed over along with my luggage, and a man took the seat next to my teammate. I eventually found somewhere to sit, only to find that my idea of personal space was not shared by my seat mates. As a man leaned into me, I perched myself on the edge of the seat with barely enough room for my arms to rest.

Then the smoking began. It seemed as if everyone on the train smoked—at least the men. My lungs were yearning for an open window. As if the smoke weren't bad enough, the pungent smell of garlic started to envelope me. I couldn't help but notice its source was sitting next to me. The man was chewing on raw garlic like a third baseman chews tobacco. Before too long, he seemed to read my mind, and opened the window. But after getting sprinkled with spit and bits of garlic, I soon realized that he wasn't so concerned with getting fresh air, he just wanted to spit the garlic out the window! I resigned myself to just sit back and take some shallow breaths for the next few hours. Near the end of the ride, I was congested and blew my nose into a tissue, only to find black soot from the smoke on the tissue. At that moment, I hoped that my next destination on this trip did not include a train ride.

I never imagined myself intentionally playing a game of chicken in any motorized vehicle, but as we were taken the next day to the orphanage by car, I was startled when our driver changed lanes and accelerated as other cars came head-on. I wasn't yet aware that it was a game of chicken, until the last minute, when one of the drivers swiftly jerked the car onto the shoulder of the road. I suppose our car "won" as we continued in the "wrong" lane and quickly managed our way back into the fast pace of traffic. I began to think that perhaps the train was not so bad after all.

We arrived at the orphanage and children were playing outdoors on a large concrete court. I was informed that I would give a lecture to fifty doctors and nurses who worked at this and other area orphanages. The director of this orphanage would bring a child to me with a disability and I would present a treatment plan for this child. The lecture was to begin in thirty minutes, and the child would be brought to me at that time. The idea of an impromptu lecture on an uncertain topic to fifty doctors and nurses made me nervous—to state it mildly—and I hoped that I would know what to say. Although I had experience with many medical problems, my experience for the past three years had been with the elderly. I prayed that my training would prepare me for this lecture.

I stood in front of the group and in walked the child. He looked quite healthy and I was told he had scoliosis, which I confirmed during my assessment. Thankfully, I had written a treatment protocol during my pediatric internship for a child with scoliosis, and the instructions for the child and the class came clearly to my mind. Calmly, I was able to demonstrate several exercises and positioning techniques to help prevent the scoliosis from worsening. I was grateful that I was able to shed some light on this problem to the boy and to the staff members.

Our group was not permitted to see any of the other children. I didn't realize that my thirty-minute session was the end of our experience at the orphanage. I learned from some of the workers that there were girls who were sickly and kept in a room together, but that our medical team was not to observe them or to give any treatment recommendations. After working with that small boy and leaving the orphanage to return to Beijing, I realized that my dream to work with the orphans in Romania had not been satisfied by this brief encounter. The desire only grew stronger. I continued to ask God to allow that desire to come to fruition.

Before we departed from Beijing, our team leader announced that he had organized a trip to see the Great Wall of China. By nature, I am not a morning person. But I was never so enthused by the idea of waking up at 5:00 a.m., in anticipation of seeing this magnificent sight, even after many difficult days of travel. The night before the trip, however, I had an intestinal flu so severe that at one point I thought I would rather die and be buried beneath the Great Wall than have to travel to see it. As I spent the night in my room lying on the cold, tile floor next to the plastic toilet, I noticed a discarded chicken bone left from the previous night's guest. This began another wave of nausea. Needless to say, I missed our group's trip to the wall. Instead, as our group traveled to see one of the world's wonders, I was confined to bed, trying to guess whether the mutton or the fish head was the culprit.

When I flew back to Colorado, my roommate Beth McElroy greeted me at the Denver International Airport. I wanted to kiss the ground before her feet, happy to see such a friendly, familiar face and happy to be back on American soil. Thankfully, my mode of transportation would not include a train filled with cigarette smoke, a van on a rocky riverbed, or a head-on game of chicken.

March 24, 2003—Age 7

While Lukas and I were playing in his bedroom, he barraged me with questions about the devil. He asked, "Is the devil's heart closed? Is his heart locked tight? He wasn't letting God get in the door of his heart. Did God transform him under heaven? Did God leave his heart? Is he going to keep his heart closed forever? Is God still standing outside his door or did God already leave? Is it like a prison underground? Could the devil dig his way up?" Needless to say, I was challenged by all of these questions, and am still not sure if I could have begun to answer them to Lukas' satisfaction. I had not talked to him about the devil, so I was surprised by his questions. More than ten years later I came upon a verse from the Bible that seemed to draw parallels with his questions. Revelation 20:1 says, "And I saw an angel coming down out of heaven, having the key to the Abyss. He seized the dragon, that ancient serpent, who is the devil, and . . . threw him into the Abyss, and locked and sealed it over him, to keep him from deceiving the nations." Lukas' questions about the

*devil weren't too far removed from the ideas that were penned
in that verse in Revelation.*

CHAPTER 9

AMAZON BY RIVERBOAT

November 2002—Age 6

Lukas and I went outside to watch the sunset, and I commented on the beautiful hues of pink and blue in the sky. He replied, "It's God's creation. God painted it with His hands."

Upon returning to Denver, I found a job at Spalding Rehab Center and delved into my work with head-injured patients. Another year passed and another letter from Operation Blessing arrived in the mail, asking if I would like to join their next medical trip. This time, the team would be traveling to Brazil to work along the Amazon River. I almost couldn't believe it. Although it was not Romania, the trip sounded so exotic that I answered the team swiftly with a resounding, "Yes."

In January 1997, our team of twelve loaded onto two small wooden boats. They were two- story—one floor for eating and the other for sleeping—and colored white with a red trim. We traveled down the Amazon just after the rainy season, which made the river murkier than I had imagined. As we traveled, I spotted my first river dolphin, with its pinkish hue, jumping out of the water. We traveled along tributaries and ended along a river bank with small wooden huts built on stilts so that they would remain intact during the deluges of rain that came and went. I saw fathers in thin canoes with their sons gathering fish in wide nets.

The sunsets were the most memorable I have seen. Maybe they were more magnificent because there were no other sounds to detract from their beauty other than those made by the birds or insects. These villagers had no cars, phones, televisions, or even radios as far as I could tell. They traveled only by boat or by foot in places where the rainforest wasn't too dense. Every village we passed had a soccer field wedged into its small space, and the boys danced with the balls between their feet. The young teenage girls helped their mothers grind corn, and many of them held babies of their own.

Most people were quite active, and their need for a physical therapist was not as dire as their need for a dentist. I worked alongside a dentist who extracted or repaired teeth on the children or adults who had succumbed to the habit of sucking on sugar cane. Although I had no experience, I quickly learned how to safely pass long, sharp instruments to the dentist, and how to say "don't be afraid" in Portuguese. At times I wondered, "Why am I here, God, when Romania still burns on my heart?" Our team was invited to go to church with the locals, and while sitting there with a young girl on my lap, God gave me a peace that in his time I would go to Romania.

During our medical clinics, held in small huts at various stops along the tributaries, my therapy skills were put to use a few times. While I worked, it was so humid, it was though I were sitting in a sauna with salty sweat dripping from me. The locals were experiencing the same steamy conditions, but didn't seem to mind. Some of the women I treated had back or shoulder pain, sometimes due to the way they held their babies while trying to work. A few of the men had back injuries due to work-related tasks. I was able to teach both groups proper carrying techniques, or body mechanics for work tasks to help prevent injury. Some of the children were eager to learn some gymnastics tricks like cartwheels, a skill every child should learn if able. The kids just laughed as I tumbled. Maybe I should have been embarrassed as I was almost thirty. But at least I had no reason to fear that my cartwheels would be featured on YouTube, as such technology was not yet invented and was certainly not a part of this culture.

Everyone in our group was getting bitten by chiggers. I escaped these bites as I was stuck on the boat one day with a violent stomach virus, the fourth member of our group to be stricken by the stomach bug. The chigger bites left red swollen boils that not only itched but remained for weeks on my comrades' arms and legs. The day after my recovery from my digestive woes, we were prepared to set-out on a hike, and I was determined to evade those nasty creatures. Fortunately, I had thought to travel with a topical bug repellent from REI, and I applied it to every inch of my legs from hip to toe. After the hike, while riding back on a small motor boat to the village where our floating house was docked, I thought I had escaped the pesky insects and the misery they bring. Soon, however, I began to feel a burning sensation on my legs. I was sitting on a metal seat, and initially thought that I was feeling the warmth from the sun's powerful heat. But the burning intensified—so much so that even the piranhas that infested the water could not deter me from diving into the river for relief. Once back on our vessel, a closer inspection showed that I had escaped the chiggers, but due to the heat from the metal seats and the bug repellent, I had chemical blisters on my legs. I am not sure which was worse.

The locals lived such simple lives, and radiated a contentedness that was so refreshing. I would eat beans and rice for a month and swim with the piranhas again anytime just to be enveloped in such serenity and raw beauty. Making our way on a tributary of the Amazon— passing father and son in their hand-carved canoe with colorful huts on stilts—I truly felt like I was part of a scene from National Geographic. However, after getting back to Colorado and reflecting on the illnesses and burns I had endured, I was content to remain stateside for a while.

CHAPTER 10

BACK IN THE USA

February 1, 2006—Age 10

One evening I was showing Lukas photographs of snowflakes taken by Wilson A. Bentley, the first man to photograph a snowflake in the late 1800s. He was also the first man to discover that there were no two snowflakes alike. He commented, "Look, God is giving us a hint. He's giving us tiny pictures and he's throwing pieces of heaven down here so we'll know what it's like in heaven. Nothing in heaven is identical."

One month after my trip to Brazil in January 1997—re-hydrated and with my intestinal flora somewhat calmed—I went skiing with a group of therapists at Arapahoe Basin in Colorado. It was a beautiful February day. Yet in the mountains, like clockwork, storm clouds started brewing overhead daily at around three o'clock. A few in the group decided they were done for the day. My friends and co-workers from Spalding Rehab—Inger Lamb, Joan Eckrich, and Karen Hookstadt, and I—took a look at the sky, with foreboding clouds rolling in, and decided they were not ominous enough to keep us from one final run on the mountain.

I was paired on a double chair with an occupational therapist named Diana Horton, an acquaintance, but the person from the group whom I knew the least. I had met her on several occasions a year prior at Mercy Hospital, as she had replaced other therapists for the day when they were sick or on vacation. As Diana and I were ascending the mountain, I asked, "What do you enjoy doing other than therapy?"

She said she was into photography, and since I had an interest in it as well, I delved a little further. I asked, "Where did you take your last photos?"

She said, "Romania."

"What were you doing in Romania?" I asked, surprised and intrigued.

"I was working in an orphanage there."

"Were you with a volunteer group?"

"Yes," she said, "I worked with a group of Swedish people from various churches in Sweden, who lived in Romania to help the orphans."

At that moment, I could feel the hair stand up on my arms against my ski jacket. When I told her that I had been trying to go to Romania for the past three years, she excitedly replied, "Oh, I can coordinate for you to work as a therapist in Romania at one of the orphanages. I have worked at a few of them, but I know the one that would work for you. It's called Casa Alba. It only has about twenty-four children, and I think it would be the best match for you."

As I looked up to the mountains before me, I knew that I would one day travel to Romania, and help at this little orphanage. I knew why the storm clouds had permitted one more ski run that day—God was opening the door to realize the vision that he had placed in my heart.

Diana continued, "Do you want to go to Romania with me this summer?"

My answer surprised me, "I just got back from Brazil, and I don't feel like the time is right." I actually didn't think I knew her well enough to explain that my digestive system had not quite recovered from my exposure to the food and water of the Amazon. We exchanged numbers and somehow I knew I would see her again.

CHAPTER 11

SUMMER OPENS THE DOOR

September 13, 2003—Age 6

Lukas said, "I am trying to believe in God even though I don't see him. How do we know that we are not just praying up to the sky?" I thought this was a poignant question for a six-year old to ask: one that comes to almost everyone at some time in their life.

Summer 1997 came and went and I thought about Diana, wondering how I could pass up an offer to go to Romania when I had waited for it for so long. But somehow I knew that I would go at the "right" time. That summer I traveled over twenty-four hours on a bus to Corpus Christi, Texas, with the youth group from my church. After playing a game of beach volleyball, I decided I needed to walk on the beach alone. Surrounded by more than 200 teenagers for five days, I needed a moment to myself. As I walked on the beach, I felt that yearning—that familiar desire to work with the children in Romania. Traveling to Kazakhstan, China and Brazil had only made me more certain that Romania was where I was meant to go. I thought of the work with teens that I had been doing in the states. Although I loved them all, I still felt the call to Romania burning in me. As I gazed at the sunset, I asked God to please allow me to go work with the children in Romania. I wondered, "Why I am having to wait so long?"

The last chapter of summer was almost finished and September had arrived. I often thought about Romania and when I would get my next chance to go. On Labor Day weekend, I met a friend named Kerri for a walk at Washington Park. When I arrived, I was so eager to walk, but she was not feeling well. We walked a short distance and decided to sit on a park bench and talk. The sun was beginning to set and we were ready to say goodbye, and I told her I was going to walk for a few minutes before I went home. She said it wasn't the best idea to walk alone, but I noticed that there were still plenty of people riding bikes and walking their dogs. She headed to her car, and I did too, but after she drove away, I felt compelled to walk. A creature of habit, I began walking my usual path around the perimeter of the park. As I made my way along my familiar route, I felt an urging, as if a voice, telling me to move off of my path for a little while, and that I would meet someone and it would change my life. Was I really about to meet someone in the next few hundred feet who would change my life? I thought, with wishful thinking, that it might be a man—preferably "the one."

At the south end of the park, I deviated from my path and followed a road on the inside of the park that wound around a lake. Again, I heard as I walked, "Change your way, stay on this path for a little while, and it is going to change your life." I had planned to make my way back to the perimeter after walking on this path for a short distance, but I continued. During the next 200-foot stretch, I looked up and saw a familiar face. It was Diana, whom I met that past February on the ski lift. She wore a shirt with the words "Romania" on the front, inside of a map of the country in the colors of its flag—yellow, blue and red. I couldn't believe it was her. I told her how I had felt directed to go off of my path and she told me she had been praying and felt she was going to run into someone she knew. Diana was not the man I had expected, but this encounter was definitely one I was grateful for!

We talked about Casa Alba, and I knew that the time was right for me to pursue this journey. She advised me to write a letter to the Swedes in Romania, explaining why I wanted to go.

That night I immediately began composing a two-page letter to the Swedish volunteers in Romania, explaining why I felt they should accept me as a therapist to work with the children. Diana gave me the contact address in Romania, and I sent my letter the next day. In November, I received the news I had eagerly awaited. I had been accepted to work at Casa Alba, the orphanage in Romania!

When I sent the letter, I didn't realize that it would take more than a month to travel to its destination. Later I was informed that the Swedes living in Romania had prayed together at a staff meeting for a therapist to come to work with the children, and they received my letter the very next day. They felt this was confirmation that I should come. I was never more ready to go.

One thing did concern me about the upcoming trip: just how would I keep my apartment in Denver, while paying to live in Romania and working there without an income? The next morning, I received a phone call from my friend Nicki (Kakos) Shier, and she asked me an interesting question. "Kristi, I haven't heard you mention Romania for a while and I was wondering, have you been accepted?" I said, "I found out this morning that I was accepted." She said, "Andy and I were praying last night and we felt led to pay your rent for the three months you will be there." I was so amazed. She and her husband felt moved before I even knew I would go, and God had guided them before they knew as well. I felt that the doors were opening before me.

I had already inquired and knew my job at Spalding Rehab could offer a three-month leave of absence, yet they couldn't guarantee my job would be there for me when I returned. It didn't matter. I knew this was the trip for which I had prayed and waited so long.

CHAPTER 12

ROMANIA AT MY FINGERTIPS

October 2002—Age 6

Lukas and I were eating dinner, and I thought I heard rain-drops. It hadn't rained in San Diego for six months, and we had been praying for rain. I asked him to go outside and see if it was raining. When I stepped outside to check for myself, I saw him, his arms outstretched, feeling the raindrops and saying, "Thank you, God. Thank you!"

My first urgent need was to find out how to get to this place called Casa Alba. Diana informed me that it was in a small village called Marghita. After consulting my atlas at home, I found that it wasn't on the map. Small, to say the least. Diana had given me a phone number to call at a house called Herculane; this was a home that housed the Swedish volunteers while they worked with the orphans in that village. I was to ask for Iorela Karlsson, a woman from Sweden who served as the director of Casa Alba. After several attempts, I finally got in touch with her and asked, "When should I come?"

She said, "If you could come a few weeks before Christmas that would be best, since there are many preparations needed for the children before the holiday. That will give me time to introduce you to the children and to the work you will do." She told me that she would be returning to Sweden for Christmas, so I would be an extra hand to help at the orphanage in her absence. She also informed me that Diana could explain how to get there, and before she hung up she said, "Oh I have one more thing to tell you. When you take the train from Budapest to Romania, you must remember to get off the train in Episcopia."

The date was set. I would leave before Christmas. It would be the first Christmas I would ever spend away from my family. As I drove toward the Denver International Airport on December 14, 1997, I turned on the radio. It was a Sunday morning and I had missed church services, so I did a channel search to see if there were any services being broadcast. When I heard a voice that seemed to be giving a message, I listened in. No more than one sentence into his message, the speaker said, "I will begin talking this morning about the word "Episcopal" from the Greek *Episkopos*, which means "one who oversees, or watches over." I didn't need to listen to another word. Episcopia was the name of the town I needed to travel to by train—the name Iorela mentioned. I knew God would be watching over me en route to this town. Little did I know how important it would be to keep this name in mind.

I flew from Denver to New York City and from NYC to Budapest, Hungary. I hadn't slept a minute and I hadn't uttered a word to the man sitting next to me on the overseas flight.

As we began our descent, I broke the silence and asked, "How long does it take a taxi to get from the airport to the train station?" He asked, "So where are you heading?"

I responded, "Romania." He asked, "Are you going there for work?" I said, "Yes, I am going to do work with the children in an orphanage."

He said, "Oh, my daughter volunteered at an orphanage there for a little while." He expressed concern, saying that when taxi drivers found out that I was an American, they would try to overcharge. He explained that he was from the Boston area and that he now lived in Budapest. He really wanted me to meet a family friend Victoria, who worked as his secretary after he brought HBO—or movies on demand—to this part of Europe. I had a feeling that he was a trustworthy person. He said, "Listen, I can give you a ride directly to the train station. Someone will be picking me up to take me to my office where you can meet Victoria. As you have a while to wait, you can have a snack and then one of us will take you to the train station." Since he mentioned a girl Victoria, and a snack, I didn't think he had a kidnaping scheme in mind, so I figured I would take him up on the offer.

After a brief meeting with Victoria at his office, I was glad I had stopped to meet her.

She offered to have me stay at her apartment for a few nights after my time in Romania was complete. I thought this was so generous, but I wasn't thinking much about the end of my trip. Victoria shed some light as to why the CEO of HBO had offered to help me. I was wearing a bulky sweater on the journey, and had been told to keep my passport unobtainable to anyone other than myself. I had my passport and travel money in a fanny pack under my sweater, and I suppose I must have looked like a swollen pear. This CEO thought that I was pregnant, and was very concerned about this pregnant woman traveling alone to a foreign country, perhaps weeks before delivery. Clearly, my more-than-bloated appearance worked in my favor. I was driven directly to the Nyugati train station in Budapest. I had made it through the first leg of my journey without a hitch. The next phase would not be so easy.

With my first step into the train station, I noticed that it was in a state of complete chaos. A commercial was being filmed, and there were lights and cameras and people everywhere. The whistling trains, footsteps of travelers and foreign words on the loudspeakers created a cacophony of sound and confusion. I walked in circles in a square room looking for signs or train tracks. Anxiously, I approached the ticket window and asked for a ticket to Episcopia. The woman behind the window sternly spoke a few terse Hungarian words and then slammed the window separating us. It may have been fortunate that I did not understand Hungarian.

My helplessness made me numb. Leaving Denver, I didn't have an ounce of fear, but now in this foreign, unforgiving place, a sense of anxiety suddenly swept over me. Not that I would have been able to converse smoothly with that terse woman, but I would have appreciated a chance to scribble the words so that she could guide me to where I needed to be. Diana had explained that the train schedule was the same every day, and I realized I was supposed to board in twenty-five minutes. But I hadn't even been able to figure out how to get a ticket. Since cell phones did not yet exist, I would not be able to call Iorela if I missed the train. I feared calling the operator in Hungary because I was sure they would hang up on me, too. Tears started to well up in my eyes, and I stood there and prayed for someone to help me amidst the noise and commotion.

In a dazed state, I walked past the cameras, glaring lights, and the meaningless hum of meaningless words reverberating throughout the large hall. I returned to a room in which I had paced back and forth in earlier. Suddenly, I noticed a man who looked Westernized and asked, "Do you speak English?" He said, "Yes, can I help you?" I said, "I need to travel to Romania." He said, "Oh, you are in the section that travels within Hungary. I will take you to the ticket booth that sells tickets for travel from Hungary to Romania." I told him I needed to get to the town Episcopia. He then spoke to a man in line and determined that he spoke Romanian, Hungarian and English. He then met a woman and found out she was traveling to a town just past Episcopia and he said, "Sit next to them and they will tell you when to get off of the train." I turned around and the Westernized man was nowhere to be found. He seemed like an apparition, and I felt indebted to this mystery man.

After buying my ticket with ten minutes to spare until the train boarded, I walked to the tracks and took a deep breath. Once on the train, men in olive suits who were armed with rifles kept storming past our train car. One group asked me a few questions and wanted to see my passport, which I handed to them, helpless to answer their questions. They were angry that I couldn't respond, but the man sitting next to me recognized that I was struggling and answered their questions for me. Thankfully, they asked no further questions. It was as though something divine was ensuring that I would make it to Romania.

Sleep escaped me during the four-hour train ride, even though I hadn't slept for a day. My trip to the "bathroom" was not very successful. I was unaware that I would need to provide my own toilet paper and that the idea of a toilet on this train was a hole in the floor with a clear view of the tracks below.

My anxiety level rose when I learned that there would be no announcements made as we approached each town, or signs informing travelers at which town the train had stopped. Passengers simply needed to know when to get off the train by the time of the stop. It didn't help that I wasn't wearing a watch. Thankfully, I sat next to a woman who was. Without the help of the woman seated next to me, I would have been riding on that train until it ran into the Black Sea! Fortunately, my timepiece angel had been "watching over me," gently tapping me on the shoulder as my stop approached, saying, "Episcopia."

CHAPTER 13

SWEDISH WELCOME TO ROMANIA

January 8, 2003—Age 7

One day, while I was driving, Lukas asked me, "How does God know everything we're thinking, and also everything everyone else is thinking?" I hesitated and wasn't sure exactly what to say. Before I had a chance to answer him, he said, "Oh, I know, he lives inside us."

I gathered my luggage and walked down the steps of the train in search of a blonde woman. There were at least ten train cars, but I found my contact standing on the platform just outside of mine.

I asked, "Are you Iorela?" She said, "You must be Kristi." We got into her car and were on our way to Marghita, home to the children of Casa Alba.

We talked non-stop for the hour long ride to Marghita. She began to tell me about how she came to find this village and about the work that I would be doing in that small orphanage. We arrived in Marghita at the Swedish volunteer house, called Herculane, as it sat on Herculane Street. I hadn't slept in the past twenty-four hours, and since the kids at the orphanage were already sleeping, I climbed into my bunk and fell asleep in an instant. The next day, I woke up feeling refreshed and unaffected by jet lag. Iorela told me she would take me to Casa Alba, and that I would stay there for about two hours before returning to Herculane. She told me I would start working the next day. I wondered why my first visit would last only two hours, but I was soon to grasp the wisdom of Iorela's decision.

During the ten minute walk to the orphanage, Iorela and I passed row after row of sterile block-like buildings with no variation in color. The air was thick and grey. Vendors worked the streets, some selling colas, others selling bread. As we walked, we passed small children begging for food. The Swedes had instructed me not to give anything to the street beggars or their demands would never cease. They had learned from experience. I hoped that I would not become insensitive to their plight, and I realized it was going to be difficult to live with myself, passing them daily with food at my disposal while they followed me with those desperate, pleading eyes.

During our walk to Casa Alba, Iorela explained how this orphanage came to exist. In 1991, a Swedish couple named Lars and Barbro Gustavsson heard about the plight of orphaned children in Romania. After traveling to Romania in 1996—and finding more than a dozen children in a hospital with scant supervision and little stimulation or interaction—the couple, along with their three children, moved to Marghita in hopes of becoming parents to the parentless. Lars developed a good relationship with the director and the head doctor at the hospital and convinced them that he could provide a more suitable place to live than a hospital room. A local man named Florin, who shared the Gustavssons' passion for the wellbeing of the orphans in his village, joined Lars in the formation of *Fundatia Crestina Elim*. Under Lar's directorship, the foundation recruited and managed locals who would be hired to provide services to the children. In collaboration with the hospital in which the orphans resided, the foundation started an orphanage that would serve as an extension of the hospital's unit for the abandoned children. They found a building that fit their needs, which happened to be white, and it was decided to name the orphanage Casa Alba, or the "White House."

After an extensive renovation to the building, fourteen children from the hospital were taken there to live. The foundation employed local Romanians to care for the children. To compliment this care, volunteers—mostly Swedes—were supplied through the foundation.

My history lesson complete, we arrived at Casa Alba, an institutional-looking white, two-story building surrounded by a black fence. I was immediately introduced to the "babies" who were from eighteen months to two years old. I fell in love with the children instantly, but had an immediate connection with one chubby, dark-haired boy with big brown eyes named Lukas. I scribed this in the first sentence of the journal I kept.

The feeling was mutual, which meant I never had to search for my new two-year old friend in the crowd. He seemed to anticipate my movements, finding his way into my lap every time I sat down. All the children craved attention—clamoring to be held, or even simply touched by a nurturing adult. They could be very demanding, and would fight for attention. Whenever one child began to cry, it started a wave, like at a football game, and almost every child would enter the chorus of wails and sobs—except for those who seemed to have retreated permanently into their own worlds.

After two hours, I was exhausted by my attempts to fill the needs of so many. I felt terribly inadequate unable to hold eight kids at a time. I now understood why Iorela thought two hours was enough for my first day.

I did not realize when I signed on as a volunteer that I would be considered a full-time worker at the orphanage and that I would be put on the schedule to do any and all tasks comprising the daily routine at the orphanage. My physical therapy sessions would need to be squeezed into stolen moments of time whenever an opportunity presented itself.

There was a meticulously organized schedule at Casa Alba, designed by Iorela. Looking back, I don't think she appreciated the brilliance of a feature of her schedule that I found refreshing—the rotation of responsibilities. In and of themselves, the housekeeping tasks were repetitive and seemed mundane, like any menial chore can be. The fact that these tasks were rotated among staff members made them not only tolerable, but at times enjoyable. After a while, I actually looked forward to an "all-nighter"—doing laundry from dusk until dawn. It was then that a few quiet moments could be found when almost all of the little ones were sleeping.

A few days after my introduction to Casa Alba, I was taken to Cadea, a town about thirty minutes away, and to the building that housed the teenage orphans there. I had not known that this place existed or would be part of my agenda during my stay in Romania, but two Swedish volunteers named Jari and Carina Manner encouraged me to go.

The teens were included in the Gustavssons' plans when—not long after the formation of Fundation Crestina Elim—the leaders realized that their services were desperately needed in surrounding regions. The foundation expanded its mission to address the needs of the abandoned from birth through the teen years, culminating in the transition to adulthood.

My visit to the teens in Cadea proved to be more emotionally draining than I could have imagined. The teenagers at Cadea lived in repulsive conditions. The rooms were not merely cold, they were freezing. Many bedrooms had broken windows, with huge gaping holes, letting the below-freezing air inside. Before setting out for Cadea, I thought I was prepared with my thermal shirt and leggings under my pants. Thankfully, Jari advised me to add some more layers, so I donned three more shirts and a guide-parka from Patagonia. Yet as I stood aghast pondering their intolerable living conditions, I was still shivering. I was so grateful for the kind gesture of a friend, Mike Williams, who had given me the thermal gear and the Patagonia jacket for the trip just before I left Denver.

The boys lived on a steady diet of potatoes and bread. I noticed that their growth had been stunted, as the size and build of the boys certainly did not match their ages. I saw one boy running down the hall to his once a week shower, a faded towel draped around his waist, exposing his torso that was ghastly thin. The next boy came running down the hall after his shower. He was fully dressed, and soaking-wet from head to toe. It was hard to fathom, but as I took in the scene before me, I realized that the shower also served as their laundromat! He stood in front of me, seemingly oblivious to the fact that he was shivering from the wet clothes that hung from his skeletal frame in the damp, frigid air. I wondered if his clothes would ever dry in this unheated building, or if he would turn into a pillar of ice before my eyes.

The air was so cold that I could see my breath as I walked down the hall. Between the inescapable chill and the institution's dismal grey color and stale smell, I asked myself if it might be more pleasant to sleep outside.

The boys had short attention spans and flitted from one topic to another. They asked me if I knew Arnold Schwarzenegger and Sylvester Stallone since I was from America. Even though they were from fourteen to eighteen, they acted more like eight-year-olds, poking at each other and teasing like school kids. They instinctively surrounded me like bees around the hive, oblivious to the concept of personal space, and some generally seemed to live in a fantasy world.

For some reason, I felt drawn to these boys. Maybe it was my experience working as a teenage youth group leader that helped me feel comfortable with them. I also felt at ease talking to them, even though I didn't understand a word they were saying. I could read it in their eyes— they craved love.

The boys lived at Cadea separated from the orphan girls, who lived a region twenty minutes away, and at first I wondered why. Lars and Barbro Gustavsson provided the answer. Barbro explained to me that they had to be separated or the girls would be taken advantage of by the teen boys— most likely in a sexual way. Lacking parental nurturing in early childhood, craving basic love and affection—with hormones surging and only one caregiver for 100 kids, how could they be expected to behave appropriately around the opposite sex?

As I walked throughout this institution, I noticed that even though the teens dressed like street urchins at times, they sometimes acquired nice things from volunteers they met or through barter. When boys who possessed such luxuries realized that their treasures would likely be stolen by other boys, they would sell the jackets or sweaters for things like cigarettes.

Some of the teens stood for hours facing a corner and rocked incessantly communicating only with a concrete wall. I wished that I could unlock their solitary minds and understand what they had endured that had sent them into this catatonic state. If only I could help them to communicate on a normal human level. A feeling of helplessness washed over me as I came to grips with the magnitude of the challenges that these boys faced.

On a trip to the restroom, I became aware that the boys had no toilet paper available to them. I learned this, of course, when I realized that there was no toilet paper available to me! The boys provided their own paper that they had to buy on the street. The bathrooms were malodorous to say the least. If I had to use it daily, I think I would have developed a new condition called "bathroom phobia." What simple things I had taken for granted for years.

KRISTI WILKINSON

October 31, 2002—Age 6

A package arrived one day from a friend of mine who Lukas knew to be seriously ill. He asked if she was getting sicker and I told him that it was possible that she would die soon. He replied, "Mom, it's God's decision when she gets to go to heaven! He could keep her here, too, if He wants," he added with a tone of disappointment. I was struck by the way he said, "gets to go" with a tone of anticipation as opposed to the way he said, "He could keep her here," clearly presenting "here" as the inferior dwelling place.

CHAPTER 14

SWEDISH STYLE CHRISTMAS IN ROMANIA

December 28, 2001—Age 6

I tried to be conservative at Christmas and not overwhelm Lukas with gifts. During his second Christmas with our family, after he finished playing with his toys, he said, "Mama, I think Santa got me too many toys. He didn't need to get me so many. Maybe we could give some of my toys to the kids without Mamas and Papas." Even though he was miles away from the children he began his life with, I knew that they remained close to him in spirit.

Since I arrived in Romania only ten days before Christmas, I had the chance to participate in an unexpected, yet wonderful task. After a day's work with the children at Casa Alba, I was taken with Iorela and another woman, Josephina, to a huge storage facility that they called "the depot." At the end of a tiring day with the kids, I was already running low on steam, but this assignment would energize me more than I could have imagined.

We began by walking into this icebox of a warehouse that felt every degree below zero that it was. It was very dimly-lit, and had ceilings that must have been forty feet high. To my great delight, our job was to pick out Christmas presents for the children. I felt like I was one of Santa's elves—albeit in a vast island of misfit toys. Perhaps the elves had taken a few months off in this village. Nevertheless, we were Christmas shopping for needy kids, and everything was free, so it was great fun. Even more fun was the prospect of finding gifts that the kids would enjoy, and we were determined to do so.

We quickly found a sea of boxes sent from Sweden, each with hygiene items and a crayon or two, and something they desperately needed—a toothbrush. Without Christmas, the children would most likely be without access to even this most basic preventive dental care.

As we began working, I remembered preparing boxes like these back in the U.S. for children in South America. I had always wondered if the boxes really ever made it to those countries, and if the children would ever get to use the items I had chosen. Here I would have the privilege of seeing the smiles on the recipients' faces. The value of a simple toothbrush was never more tangible to me.

We each went through at least 100 boxes, with barely enough light to see what they contained, or to find items that would complement those already chosen. I felt as though I were swimming through piles of used clothes in a super-sized Salvation Army before anyone had time to place the garments on a hanger. Truckloads of items had been brought from Sweden to this village to help provide for the children. As I sifted through the clothes, the faces of the children appeared before me in my mind's eye as I tried to find something for each of them to wear on that special day.

Unfortunately, there were too many gifts to sort through in this dark, frigid building. Thankfully, Iorela decided that we should take a few bags of gifts back to Casa Alba where we could choose the gifts for each child. After all, it was close to midnight.

The next day, Josephina and I got an early start sorting out two toys each for each child. Before coming to Romania, I thought that the pace would not seem as hectic as in the U.S. But with twenty-four kids to "shop" for, I felt that same mix of pressure and anticipation that I always felt back home during the holiday season. Some of the toys we had to choose from had words scratched off, some were dirty, some were missing parts, like an ear or boots. These were the gifts available to us, so I tried not to feel disappointed for the recipients. After a few hours, we had our gifts and outfits ready and would be prepared for the celebration to begin.

On Christmas Eve, the children woke from their afternoon naps to find a "new" outfit to wear for that evening's celebration. The Swedes knew how to celebrate Christmas! For two days, male and female staff members alike had been baking breads and pastries that were braided and twisted into the most magnificent pieces of dough I had ever seen. They were also geniuses with gingerbread and had three-story houses and cookies ready for the evening. The biggest room in the orphanage was made into one grand eating room, with the tables arranged so that all twenty-four children could eat together at one big table. Swedes generally eat candy and sweets only on Saturdays, avoiding them all other days for health reasons. This custom was passed on as part of the routine at the orphanage as well. But Christmas Eve was cause for making an exception. Staff members filled a large bowl with candies in which the children could indulge freely. It was a feast. I can still picture the chocolate dripping from some of the mouths and smeared across their ruddy cheeks, as they cheered, "Bomboane, bomboane!" (Candy, candy!). That was the children's favorite day of the Christmas season for sure.

I sat near Lukas during the holiday feast, and held him just after he received his gift of a gently used sweater that he could wear on special occasions. I felt compelled to spend as much time with him as possible, even though I had at least three other children in my care.

After the plates were cleared, Barbro's husband Lars Gustavsson— father to hundreds in spirit—assumed the role of Father Christmas. He appropriately wore Santa's red suit. His size and rotund stature were perfect for the role, but the children did not recognize him at first, tugging on his suit as he walked in carrying the gifts. The excitement in their eyes was beyond description as they heard their names called to receive their individual gift. I noticed that they did not care that the toys and clothes had been used, broken or torn—so different from the disappointment an American child may demonstrate upon receiving tattered toys from a second-hand store.

One child named Karcsi, (pronounced "Kochee") had a touching and memorable response to a key ring I had bought in the states and gave to him. I can still hear his little voice saying, "keye," "keye," as he clung to his gift. He took great care to ensure that no one else would touch his new keys, and staff no longer had to wonder where their own keys had wandered as they prepared to head home for the evening. He went to bed that night with his keys by his side, as he did every night that followed.

My heart was saddened by a six year old girl named Silvia at Casa Alba. She had been in the first group of fourteen children to arrive at the orphanage. Unfortunately, the neglect she endured before her time at Casa Alba led to what I would describe as an institution-based autism. "Speech" for her consisted of strings of nonsensical words, and her form of "play" was demonstrated by an obsession with ripping paper into tiny shreds. She was very satisfied with the gift I chose for her that Christmas, which included pages of paper that she could tear to her heart's delight.

After the kids enjoyed their gifts and fell asleep, the Swedes had an evening meal and then everyone went back to Herculane to watch Disney cartoons, as was their Christmas Eve tradition. I found it interesting that the Swedes watched American cartoons that I had never seen, and thought I might adopt a new tradition upon returning to the states. On Christmas Day, the traditional Swedish meal consisted of meatballs, herring, hard-boiled eggs, and a variety of cheeses. After so many challenges with foreign cuisine, I was more than ready for a feast like this!

That night in my bunk bed, I read Luke's version of the Christmas story in the Bible. It might be familiar to some from watching Charlie Brown. In that Christmas classic, Linus refers to that chapter when he talks about an angel of the Lord, shepherds in the fields, and a child wrapped in swaddling clothes, lying in a manger. Something stood out for me for the first time when I read that chapter in Luke. After Jesus' birth, the verses mention that a pair of turtle doves were given as an offering, when he was to be presented to the Lord. I didn't realize that turtle doves were mentioned in the Bible and that those two doves had also woven their way into the song I had sung for thirty years, "The Twelve Days of Christmas" with five golden rings, three french hens, two turtle doves, and a partridge in a pear tree. I went to sleep with thoughts of the two doves sitting in that pear tree.

On Christmas morning, I had a strange ache in my heart, and came to realize that I was feeling the absence of my own traditions at Christmas time. This year I hadn't attended a Christmas Eve service, didn't go to door to door in the neighborhood singing carols, didn't sing "Silent Night" during a candlelight service or watch the annual Christmas Eve pageant. There were no boxes to open under a tree or stockings hung by the chimney.

In this state of mind, I went to work at Casa Alba. I savored the time with the few children who remained at the orphanage with nowhere else to celebrate. The others, including Lukas, went to the homes of the Romanian employees for one or two days to celebrate the holiday.

I had a deep sadness in my heart, knowing that I would not be able to be with the child I had felt so drawn to on Christmas day. But I was happy that another caregiver wanted to give him that special attention that he needed. I began to daydream about taking Lukas home with me one day, but knew this was only a dream.

The Romanian workers at Casa Alba embraced the children in their care as if they were their own. I was so touched that so many of them, especially two women, named Monica and Ligia, took children home on their days off from work during this holiday, and on other days as well. They received no pay for this or no accolades from anyone, they simply knew that it was the best thing for the children. I could sense the love of the people of Romania in general for children—a love that could not be strangled by the tyrant Ceausescu or the poverty that paralyzed many after his regime.

Josephina and I were the only people from the Swedish house to work at Casa Alba that day. It was nearing dinner time, and we were standing in the kitchen, preparing tea for some of the kids. As I looked out through the window curtained in red and white, I noticed two turtle doves, perched on a tree limb outside. The pair seemed to sit peacefully, looking at us and then to the street. I truly knew those two doves were a blessing from God, just as I had discovered them in the book of Luke the night before. They sat on that branch to let me know I was not alone, and that His gift of the Christ child would be a treasure who would be with me always. This was my most memorable and sacred Christmas gift, and a moment that I will always treasure.

CHAPTER 15

RING IN THE NEW YEAR

March 6, 2005—Age 9

We were in the car and as I was driving Lukas said, "I have a word, Mama. It's like we're living in heaven's basement. Just like things in a basement are junky, we are junky and then He restores us in heaven." I know he hadn't heard this in the classes we volunteered for in church, and certainly not in his public school.

New Year's Eve was approaching, and on this misty day, I decided to go on one of many walks in the small agrarian village. As I walked toward a train station, I passed an old train car that appeared to have been stranded by the tracks for fifty years. I turned down another street, or so it was called, that barely had any "street" left to it. It had piles of dirt and concrete every five to ten feet, as if someone had been there recently to salvage the road, but had long since forgotten the task. Every other step on the street had to be watched lest I sink into a deep pothole, as if a strange beast had taken large bites out of it. The houses mimicked the road in its tattered state. They were like small square boxes, 400 square feet if they were lucky, with paint chipping from the walls, and roofs that caved or curved, barely insulating the people within.

I followed a canal with a grass walkway, and rain started to fall, making the air seem more fresh and clean than usual. As I gazed to my right, layered hills blanketed the landscape below, and patches of light cast shadows on mounds of haystacks. Next to the haystacks stood a cart-like buggy that seemed ready for harvest, lacking only a farmhand to do the work. A flock of crows sat on a barren tree branch, squawking that they, too, would need food before too long. In the distance, a large church, called the "basilica," stood in a stately way. With its silver steeple rising into the clouds, it looked almost as if one were an extension of the other. Beams of light shone on that steeple, showing me that beauty still existed in this depressed land. I should have felt alone, as no one could fully communicate with me in this village. Yet I felt that God had met me there on that path.

Though I was uncertain where I was going, I walked onward as it seemed calming to me. I came upon a road untraveled by cars that wound upward until I reached a point where I could see all of Marghita. Before me were green and brown patches of farmland, rows of fruit trees, and what appeared to be a small orchard. All of this scenery was in a town that was trying to rebuild itself, but remained broken in so many ways. After I wound my way back down the hill and walked along the canal again, I passed two sheepherders lazily directing their flock of sheep, which were busy grazing on the grass on the hillside. It was as though I had stepped back in time.

New Year's Eve arrived, and I must say it was unique to say the least. A co-worker at the orphanage named Petri asked me if I would like to join him for church. He was from Marghita and also was wonderful with the children. Since I had never been to church on New Year's Eve, I thought it would give me a new perspective on services in this village. He walked me home to Herculane the previous day, even though I insisted I had done this alone with no problem. I thought something was peculiar. He was only eighteen, and as I was thirty, I had no thought that he could remotely be interested in me. People told me I looked young for my age, but I figured he knew how old I was. I gave him a few excuses as to why I couldn't go, but they didn't seem to work. Because of his unyielding persistence, I decided to go—after all, it was just a church service.

Petri picked me up at 6:30 p.m., sharp for a 7 p.m., service, and we walked several blocks before he asked, "May I?" asking to walk arm in arm. Thinking this was just a Romanian nicety so that a lady would not trip on the uneven streets, I didn't make anything else of it. We walked to the church entrance and received the first of several stares from his teen-aged friends. He told me that he played the keyboard and that he would be in the front of the church during the whole service. That meant I would be sitting alone. But that didn't matter as the boys would sit on one side and the girls and women the other, as is traditional in this village. I received a few more awkward stares as he gave them a wink from his place at the keyboard, and when I took a quick look behind me, I couldn't help but notice that almost every teen was glancing my way, silently saying, "Just who is this blonde foreigner here with Petri?"

The service began. Although Petri said it would last about two hours, those two hours came and went and the crowd remained. The room didn't seem to be heated, and was freezing. I tried to sit on my hands to keep them warm, but this didn't work as the bench seemed like a block of ice to me. It didn't help that women had to wear skirts at church. I wasn't wearing any leggings or stockings under my skirt, and my thigh muscles tensed, and then became numb. A moldy smell seemed to hover near me, and to distract myself from the cold and the stench, I started to count the number of songs that were sung. I counted to song number twenty-five, all of which were unfamiliar to me. Finally the children's choir sang a tune I recognized—how comforting it was to be met with the familiar. Other than that sweet song, I hadn't understood a word and wouldn't for the following four to five sermons and forty additional prayers, interspersed among the many songs.

My bladder was about to burst, but I knew that even if I had the nerve to get up, I wouldn't have known where to find the bathroom. Some of the songs extended to as many as six verses. Just when I thought I couldn't bear another moment, they all agreed that they must repeat one of the pastor's favorite songs. It reminded me of a time when I was in third grade, and was taken to visit distant elderly relatives, with conversation floating endlessly around me. I prayed and prayed, but not with thanks for the New Year—I earnestly prayed for the service to end. I felt so awful, being that I was in the Lord's house, but my body couldn't stand another minute. Finally, I think God listened and they sang Happy Birthday to the New Year, which had at least four verses. After three long hours, the service ended.

Petri walked me home and again asked, "May I?" I started to get a bit suspicious. I decided to steer the conversation to topics about high school, and asked what grade he was in, hoping he would ask me the same. He asked my age, a question I couldn't wait to answer. When I said, "Thirty," he said, "Scuzatz," which I understood as "excuse me,"—as if I was mistaken or if I didn't understand his question. I insisted that I was thirty, and that his English was good enough for me to follow. Suddenly, he blurted out a nervous laugh and said, "My mom is thirty-nine. She doesn't look your age." I knew his mother, and didn't want to say I agreed, even though I did. I was so relieved that he knew we would not be an "item." I had to laugh later that night when it was confirmed by Louise and Angelica—two Swedish volunteers who lived with me—that walking arm in arm was not just a gentlemanly Romanian thing to do; it was considered a big deal here.

I will admit that I wasn't eager to return to church again any time soon. However, on the next day at work, Petri's mother insisted—just as her son had—that I take the kids from Casa Alba to church for the New Year's Day Celebration. So off I went with Karsci, Valentin, and Josef. Those kids had to sit through two-and-a-half hours of church. It wasn't a mystery why Karsci wanted to go "kaka" more than twice during the service. I wouldn't have minded staying in the bathroom playing with the water in the sink with him, but knew others might start to notice our absence. It wouldn't have been so bad if the girl sitting next to me—who was kindly trying to interpret the service for me—hadn't eaten garlic for her last meal, as was commonplace in this country. I tried to turn my head away from her, as if I had discovered an angle that made her words more audible to me. With relief, I noticed that some people were leaving the service early. Grateful to be sitting inconspicuously in the rear of the church, I followed suit. Karsci, Vali and Josef and I went on a nice walk. Or so it began.

Many people shared the road we traversed on this busy holiday, and it seemed a custom to attend church that day. I was doing my best to keep the three boys in tow. All of a sudden Josef decided to throw off his coat and pull down his pants in the middle of the street. He did this just as a flock of people were making their pilgrimage to church. If his nudity weren't bad enough, he let out a blood-curdling shriek and refused to stand. Those walking by, who knew by the way I was dressed that I was a foreigner, must have thought I was the worst girl for the job. It seemed like an exasperating way to ring in the New Year. Just then Josef agreed to pull up his pants, and the four of us strolled back to Casa Alba as we sang the only Romanian song I knew (it was sung before every meal) "Multsumesc pentru mun care, multsumesc pentru casa mia." It meant, "Thank you God for giving us food, thank you God for giving us a house," and it ended, "Hallelujah, Amen." I could say Amen to that!

We got back to Casa Alba and started the nightly ritual of pajamas, followed by the brushing of teeth. Trying to get twenty-four kids to go to sleep at once seemed like an impossible task. As soon as one would get a surge of energy, pandemonium would seem to rise, only to be quelled by Iorela. She would create an impromptu puppet show, or sing a song about the large moon and the small stars, along with hand gestures, and a calm would wash over all the children.

CHAPTER 16

THE YELLOW ROOM

Summer 2000—Age 4

We were at the park and Lukas saw a very pregnant woman. He then asked me, "When you have a baby, will I have to go away?" I told him that I would never send him away, that he would be my son forever. He then asked, "What do you think you will name the baby? Can you ask God what the name is now?"

After the New Year I was assigned to a room with the youngest children, named Adina, Lavinia, Lukas and Gusztav. As a way of distinguishing one group of children from another, each room was given the name of a color, and mine was the "yellow room." After keeping the kids busy all day and using the tricks I learned from experienced staffers, I would finally get the children into their cribs. Then one would try to climb out of his or her crib, or would stand and rock, showing no signs of tiring. Finally, after I sang them a few songs, everyone would be quiet and I would find myself lying on the floor, more ready to collapse than any of the children.

Adina was an angry little girl. She was quite cute, but wore the biggest frown on her face that could be considered a scowl. Her mother lived in a nearby town, and I think this is what fueled her anger—Adina knew this as well. Adina's mother or an aunt would come to Casa Alba, pick her up for a few days, and then bring her back to be cared for by the staff. Adina had a sadness in her eyes that seemed to ask, "why do they keep leaving me here?" Although I tried to get her to warm up to me, her shell had already hardened, and I wasn't going to be the one to break it, despite my best efforts.

Lavinia was two, but developmentally she moved as if she were only six months old. She sat with her head and trunk slumped forward, couldn't stand, and had trouble holding her head up when lying down. This was all because she had spent too much time lying in a crib, untouched. She was the reason I was assigned to that room; as I worked with the children, I could focus attention on improving her movements when I found time. We spent many mornings and afternoons on a rug, and an exercise ball that was brought in from Sweden. Her expressions were dull, and she did not communicate verbally or even attempt many sounds. She did, however, let me know that she did not like the positions I tried to get her to assume, which were to strengthen that weak little torso of hers. She had eyes that were so dark they were almost black, which matched her hair. Her eyes were wide and wandering. I wondered if she would ever develop the strength to stand or walk, and if I would ever get to witness that first step.

Lukas was two, and was so precious that I was instantly drawn to him. He had brown almond eyes that had either a sparkle or a tear welling on the brim and ready to fall. He craved being held, and I found myself either holding him by my side or carrying him on my back. He always found my lap, and would turn and sit before he checked to see if I would remain seated. He wanted my undivided attention and would only reluctantly share it with one person, Gusztav—his best friend.

Gusztav was also two and was a beautiful child, with eyes like those of a baby seal—so big you felt you could swim in them. He had a warm spirit and a warm place in his heart for Iorela, whom he followed everywhere. If she was gone, he would let me carry him side by side with Lukas. But if he knew she was working at Casa Alba, he would find her and would help her as she worked in her office, or swept the kitchen, or organized twenty-five pairs of shoes.

I spent most days with these four children, unless we rotated and I would be assigned to work a group of toddlers or with the four-year-old boys. The toddlers included boys named Otto, Imre, and Csaba. This four-year-old group included Karcsi, Valentin, and Josef, and a little boy named Craciun, which meant Christmas in Romanian. I loved these boys as well, and loved it even more when Karsci would yell, "Kristi, Kristi" down the hall when he would see me. Lukas seemed to be paying attention and would call out 'Kitty, Kitty," as he couldn't quite pronounce the rolling "r" in my name the way the older boys did in that country.

I was often matched to work at Casa Alba on the morning shift with a woman named Inci, who was from Marghita. She took care of another group of toddlers in the room next door which also housed four children. We shared a task that I believed would take us weeks, perhaps months: potty training. There were eight children that all needed to be transitioned into using the toilet and I knew authors like Dr. Spock wrote entire chapters in books about this. How could we accomplish this with so many strong-willed kids?

When it came to potty training, Inci could be compared to a fairy godmother. In the morning shortly after breakfast, she lined up eight blue portable potties on the bathroom floor. The children called these little potties the "olitza." Inci sternly told all four of her toddlers to sit down on their little "olitzas" and gestured to me to do the same with the four from the "yellow" room. To my amazement, all eight children sat quietly, one or two occasionally rising from their perch, only to be emphatically told by Inci to return to their posts. We repeated this after every meal and after nap time, with each child just inches from the other. I noticed that it seemed innate to them to copy the behavior of their peers. They sat obediently and gazed left to right to make sure that their friends had all remained seated. If one child was successful, Inci and I would cheer for that child and raise our hands in the air to compliment them on this huge success. All of the children would imitate us, hands waving wildly, wanting to be applauded as well. To my utter amazement, we had successfully potty-trained all of the children in one week—except one little girl with developmental delays, who I felt may never fully understand the use of the "potty." Mothers from around the globe would have been envious of how quickly we completed this childhood milestone. I will always be awestruck by Inci's touch of magic when it came to the "olitza." Even Dr. Spock would have marveled at this feat!

Whether I was with the two or four-year-olds, I tried to take them outside at every given opportunity. Some of the younger Romanian work-ers were happy to join me with the children. One young woman from Marghita named Monica was one of them. We would bundle the kids up in their winter suits, and set off for walks throughout the village. However, our efforts were quickly denied if Lenutsa or Florica—two of the more seasoned caregivers—noticed that it was a bit cold outside. Kids here were forbidden to go outdoors in these conditions, for fear that they would become sick. Having a science background, I wanted to tell them that one doesn't catch a cold from the cold. However, I could tell by their stern expressions that I wasn't going to change years of superstition, a supersti-tion still held by many in the U.S. If a child so much as sneezed, that was it—they would be kept inside. So, if it was considered too chilly—which was almost every day in the winter—and I wasn't allowed to take the kids outside to play, I had them do gymnastics in the playroom. I had done gymnastics throughout my youth, and by demonstrating the moves, I found I got as much exercises as they did. Of all the children, Karcsi loved "gymnastika" the most, and I would send him flipping in the air again, again and again. He wore maroon and white striped leggings every day that worked so well with handstands and somersaults. He was dismayed when he outgrew them and reluctantly handed them down to a younger child.

After gymnastics at Casa Alba, I was sitting on a chair with the "older" children, and Karcsi and Gusztav were perched on my lap. Lukas fell and was crying, wanting me to pick him up and hold him in my arms. Valentin looked at him and then noticed that I had my hands full, so Vali went to Lukas and lay on the floor next to him, and stroked his head and his arm, comforting him. That expression was so priceless and humbling—to see a four-year-old comfort a younger child as an adult would. It was obvious that Valentin was such a bright, sensitive child. I prayed for a family to find him, who he could call his own.

October 15, 2005—Age 9

Our cat Simba disappeared, and Lukas searched for him for days. He and a few of his neighborhood friends drew and posted signs, asking if anyone had seen him. Coyotes are known to roam our area, and Lukas needed closure—to know whether Simba was dead or alive. He looked out the window and said, "Mom, I saw a light shadow of Simba and then it was gone. Then a leaf rolled across the street showing me he was gone. The leaf was being batted around like Simba was playing with it, but there was no wind to move the leaf. I was the one God showed the shadow to because I was sad. He ends up with one million—like all of the cats and catnip in heaven—and we end up here with zero."

CHAPTER 17

THE GIRL WITH THE ALMOND-EYES

September 2004—Age 8

Lukas was in first grade and it was back to school night. I had not yet formally met his teacher, Mrs Piddington, and when I came into the class, she said, "Are you Lukas' mom?" I said that I was and she said, "Well, I want you to look at this self-portrait. I have been teaching for twenty years and I have not had one like it." Since Lukas drew all the time, when I looked at the pictures the kids had drawn of themselves, I knew instantly which was his. His self-portrait featured a sad face, with tears streaming down the cheeks. He also drew his heart and veins and vessels and other organs. I went up to Mrs. Piddington and she remarked, "When I asked Lukas why he had tears in his picture, he said, 'Everyone was teasing me because my picture looked different, so I was sad and I drew tears. But I wanted you to see me from the inside out.'" Thus the explanation for the heart and organs and vessels drawn on his self portrait. Now I knew why she had not seen one quite like it.

There is a gypsy population in Marghita, and I didn't know what that really meant until I lived there. Most of the gypsies in Marghita beg on the streets or send their children to beg for them. They are considered outcasts and most Romanians won't employ them for work. Their homes aren't typically in the same area as the other Romanian homes, but are situated just beyond the periphery. I could feel the tension in the space between the two classes like the invisible force of two magnets repelling each other.

In my first weeks in Romania, I formed an unfair judgment in my spirit. Having noticed that most of the children at Casa Alba were of the gypsy class, I quickly developed an attitude of condemnation toward the mothers and fathers for giving up their children. I thought, *How could a mother give away her child*? I just couldn't fathom why they would do this. I soon got a glimpse as to why.

Walking was my outlet in this town, and it is safe to say that I walked hundreds of miles while there. Unfortunately on certain days I would gear up with layer upon layer of clothing, but after a few minutes, I would need to head back to Herculane. There were no restrictions on the cars or factories to keep the air from being polluted. Because of this, I would often forego my walk as I felt that I was being asphyxiated by the smoke that hovered around and above me. But, on clear days when the air was clean and the sun made its way beyond the clouds, I put my shoes through the wringer on those muddy streets.

My walks would often take me to the edges of the town, and I would sometimes wander into places where I was not welcome. On one such occasion, I happened upon two gypsy communities. I made my way as close to their homes as I felt I could without being considered a trespasser, hoping to learn a little about their lifestyle.

After a rainfall, the water that fell on the muddy streets carved ripples into the road that then became eroded fissures, making the roads impassable by car. This was not an issue for the gypsies as they did not own vehicles. They would travel on foot until they reached their typical mode of transportation—covered wagons. I had seen these in history books and on *Little House on the Prairie*, but I didn't think they were still being used, even in third-world countries.

As I walked past the houses, which were little more than huts, I noticed that they were made of handmade mud bricks, stacked to form dwellings just over five feet high, with ten by ten foot interiors. This was it—this was all the space they had. These primitive homes had no electricity, no heat, no lights, no toilets inside. I didn't even see anything that could be considered an outhouse. They burned most of their trash in a heap, which left a sickening odor in the air. The rest of their trash did not make it into the fire, but had been simply tossed aside and lay strewn along the road.

On one of my walking trips to the dismal outskirts of town, it was a chilling twenty degrees. As I walked, I tried to imagine the feeling of arriving home and not finding relief from the cold. I tried to imagine not having access to a warm bath in the winter or the simple pleasure of hot chocolate after a sled ride. The gypsies couldn't find work in the villages as prejudice against them ran deep. Realizing this, it was hard not to feel respect and compassion for them. I had come to understand that when a gypsy family gave up a child, it was an act of desperation—the only option they had to provide a better life for their child. If I lived in this village and couldn't find food for my fourth or fifth child, I might decide, like they did, to give up my child to someone who could provide a warm, safe home. My understanding broadened, and I dropped that hardened shell of judgment for the women who brought their children to the orphanage in hopes that they would get the care they needed.

One day, just a few steps outside the gate at Herculane, a gypsy girl that I had seen before caught up with me. She insisted that I give her some food, but I didn't have any food or money with me. I had been warned not to give anything to the gypsies or they would just keep begging for more.

I let her know that I didn't have anything to give to her, but to my surprise she kept walking with me. After walking for about ten minutes, she took my hand. We walked hand-in- hand for an hour, through barren, yet wonderful apple trees. I couldn't help but notice that the hand I was holding was swollen and red, and her fingernails looked worn and cracked. Each finger joint looked as if it would break if I held her hand more firmly. Her hands resembled those of my elderly patients.

We were able to communicate using my limited Spanish—the words I knew were similar to Romanian words. I had learned them from several Spanish-speaking patients I treated while in Denver, and was so grateful that these words had allowed me to communicate with her also.

I found out that her name was Ashbeta. She was twelve and had at least ten siblings, and lived in a meager home just past Casa Alba, in one of the villages I had just discovered. She was so striking—one of the most beautiful gypsy girls that I had seen, with hazel-brown eyes that sparkled when she spoke. I looked at her and told her in Romanian that Jesus loved her—words we said every day at mealtime at the orphanage. She understood and told me she knew He loved her. Knowing this eased my feelings of sadness for her living conditions.

As we walked, I felt we could communicate silently at times, more deeply than I could communicate with some people in English. I felt a love for her coming through my hands, and I could feel it from her in return. She smiled during the entire walk as she held my hand in the damp, cold air, and through the wind that swept over the hillside. I also noticed that her legs—about the size of my forearms—appeared stick-like in her thin red pants. While she walked, her knees remained in a slightly bent position which indicated a deformity. Since the joints in her hands appeared arthritic, I guessed that her knees were as well. I wondered if, at her young age, her joint issues had been caused by life in a poorly built home, too many winters without relief from the cold, winds wafting through the cracks that were common in the walls of gypsy homes.

Nearing my "home," I realized I had nothing much to give her other than a few cashews that I found in my pocket. This seemed like such an insult after our walk, but she welcomed them and ate them instantly. She now knew I cared for her, and I had the sense that she valued this more than any food I could have given to her. I will never forget Ashbeta and the brief time we spent. Her wide smile and almond brown eyes will be etched in my mind and heart forever. She taught me more than humility. She taught me how someone with so little could still experience joy.

CHAPTER 18

BITTERSWEET JANUARY

June 2, 2009—Age 13

Lukas and I were talking and he said, "If people without faith blame God, then they actually believe. Everyone believes, some are just clouded."

It was January 1998, I had been in Marghita for a month, which seemed at times, like forever, and at other times like a quick blur. I had decided to go for a walk when suddenly a feeling of dread overwhelmed me. I wanted to hop on a plane and leave for home that very moment—almost as if I had been banished to this unforgiving country. My feelings stemmed not only from the plight of the children, but also the frigid, damp and dismal climate.

I set out on my daily walk, despite the toxic feel of the atmosphere that day. Against my better judgment, I kept walking as my chest and lungs burned from the thick, polluted air. I needed the walk to clear my mind. In addition to my feeling of dread, I felt that I needed insight for a meeting the volunteers were having that evening. I asked God to give me this insight.

I found an unfamiliar street that I had not yet traversed. I approached a bread factory, and watched smoke billow out of the chimney like one of the geysers at Yellowstone. Instead of the aroma of fresh bread, my nasal passages were filled with dusky gray fumes. As I had feared, it seemed that the damage to my lungs would likely outweigh the benefits of the walk.

Raindrops started to fall on my cheeks and eyelashes, and I looked down at my feet. My shoes were dirty, the cars passing me were dirty—even the rain was dirty. It was as if God were crying, and the raindrops that fell were stained with his sadness—I felt that He cried for the children as I did.

Beyond the factory cloud, yet another overwhelming stench filled the air. This had a repulsive, smoky smell that replaced the chemical one. And then I saw "it" in the middle of the street—a plump pig, with its entrails inside-out. Its skin, once a nice pinkish color, was now charcoal black, as it had just been charred. I suppose the neighbors were preparing dinner and the street provided the perfect place for slaughter. This walk was a far cry from the one I had taken the day before, when the sun was shining and the air was crisp and refreshing.

In an attempt to leave these horrid smells behind, I continued toward a familiar orchard. Not far up the hillside, I noticed the sound of a tractor plowing its way through the thick, hard dirt between the rows of apple trees. I couldn't see the tractor, I could only hear its humming sound. I knew that it was doing its work in the middle of the winter, preparing the earth to nourish the trees. I considered how those trees had rested and had been still all winter long, and how this tractor's work was necessary, even though winter seemed an odd time for farm work. Yet, it was crucial for each tree, and the work of the tractor prepared the tree to flower and to be more fruitful during growing season.

My eyes scanned up and down the hills for this tractor. Even on my return home, I knew it was there in the field, but could not see it. I felt as though this was just as God wanted me to picture it: His hand is at work, but is not always seen. And just when we believe He is not at work and has forgotten us, He is preparing the road and a plan for us. This work may be done at a time when we hadn't anticipated it, but the work in the winter is necessary for us to flourish and grow in the springtime. Before I started on this walk, I thought that perhaps He had forgotten these children in this small village. But I realized that these children were just like the trees. He was doing a work in them that I could not see now—preparing their minds and bodies to heal, just as he touched the trees.

August 21, 2005—Age 9

One night Lukas was playing with Legos and he stopped and said to me, "God is giving me a thought." This night, he had several pictures he wanted to describe. I had a hard time understanding him at first, and had to ask him to repeat certain parts. He began with these words, "We are all warriors, but God has special powers kind of like Superman. He's the one with the suit made of gold and everyone else has regular armor on. He's got the best castle made of gold."

A moment later he was envisioning a picture of a tree that he wanted to describe to me. He said, "Do you know the trees that are old? We're the old, icky, black, burnt down trees, but He's the tree made of gold. His tree stem is big and glorious and sturdy. When you sin, and you do those things again and again that you don't want to do, your old black bark falls off the tree; you're not part of the tree. But when you accept Jesus, the black bark becomes gold like His. Every line on the tree represents every person in the universe. The line disappears and falls off when someone sins.

"It's like God's losing one of His glorious leaves or lines on the tree that He made; it's kind of like He lost one of the rooms He prepared in heaven. When you ask for forgiveness, that leaf or bark that fell to the ground pops back onto the tree, and the person's line comes back onto the tree and your room in heaven is given back to you." Then he said, "I think you are supposed to write this and tell people. You may not understand because you don't have the gift from God, but you have other gifts that I don't have, so don't worry."

I didn't know what to think after this. For those who wonder if he had read this somewhere, I can assure that he absolutely had not! Lukas has severe dyslexia, and up to that point he could not read independently. He had never heard this at church or school. I had never talked to him about any of these ideas. I really didn't understand what he was saying at first because his

thoughts were coming so quickly. When I asked him about it,
he said no one had told him this, he just heard it from God.

CHAPTER 19

THE CADEA BOYS

April 2, 2006—Age 10

Lukas and I were at a church in Escondido, and the sermon was on faith and trust. The minister used the metaphor of walking on a tightrope, like that of trusting God so that we would not fall. Lukas was doodling and then he whispered to me, "I have a thought. The Devil's Bible is the Devil's own grave." He then waited a few minutes and had more to share. He whispered again saying, "We're supposed to go to heaven to have one more person for God's army. Then the Devil goes down, down— lower and lower—and there are less people going to him. The Devil's little demons are like pieces of sand around him." I asked him what he meant by the sand and he said, "A piece of sand is like nothing compared to God's army that is like the sand of the seashore." He paused and added, "When the Devil and God meet face to face, the Devil will go down to the pit of flaming fire. He (the Devil) tries to say he's prince, or king, but he isn't."

I asked Lukas about these thoughts since I had never told him anything about the Devil, except in response to questions he may have asked about the subject. He already struggled with anxious thoughts and I didn't want to give him more reason to worry. He said to me, "God gives me these thoughts. He speaks them to my brain as I listen to him. Sometimes I get them everyday, but I don't always tell you." I had never imagined an army in heaven, and didn't like to focus on the details of Hell. He would tell me about these things at random times—when we were driving, playing with Legos, or going for a walk. Sometimes even I didn't want to think about some of the things he talked about, especially demons—something I certainly never mentioned to him.

I returned to Cadea—the orphanage for the teenaged boys—with Jari and Cari, a Swedish couple who lived in the bunk room with me at the volunteer house. A swarm of boys buzzed in around us, and Emeric was there to greet me. They wanted their photographs taken. As they gathered arm in arm—smiling ear to ear as Carina took their picture—I couldn't help but notice their tousled hair and dirty hands. Their smell reminded me that they only had warm water to shower once a week. As I looked at Emeric, something concerned me. He smiled for the camera, while sucking his finger, without a care that he was being photographed. This would have seemed quite natural for the kids at Casa Alba, but Emeric was sixteen! He then grabbed my hand and held it tightly while we walked behind another group of boys as they eagerly headed to dinner. I sat at the table with Emeric on metal chairs, and it was that meal that changed my life forever. Disturbed by my thoughts, I couldn't sleep that night. I tossed and turned and finally got out of bed at two in the morning, and sat on my bunk in the pitch dark. With my flashlight in one hand, I penned my thoughts with the other in a poem of sorts.

In His Hands

I stepped inside the building. It was called "home."
Home for one hundred teenage orphan boys,
maybe more, but who was counting?
It was dimly lit, but I could see their faces.
I walked down a long corridor and
the cold air ran through me.
I could see their breath as I walked.
Within seconds ten, perhaps twelve
boys were hovering around me.

They spoke to me so quickly, and although
I couldn't understand the words,
the meaning was in their eyes.
They wanted to leave this place they called
home, but it was the only home they knew.
He ran to me with a smile and open arms,
as if he had not seen me for years,
so hungry for attention, yet he barely knew me.
His eye was black and blue again. Perhaps he
had a pair of shoes someone else wanted.
He reached out to shake my hand. I hesitated.
A part of me didn't want to touch his dirty hand again.
He stood close to me and his odor
was amost too strong to bear.
His clothes were ragged and torn,
so covered with filth, just like all the other boys.
He walked to one room, but he was pushed
from the door. He could not enter.
There was a pecking order here,
and he was not at the top.
He led me to his room which he
shared with five other boys.
His bed was bare, without anything to cover
it. Each blanket had to be locked away
until nighttime or else it would be stolen by someone older and stronger.
There were pictures on the walls drawn by
the boys of a life in their dreams.
They were of beaches with palm trees, the
sea and the sky, drawn in three layers,
like something I'd seen in a third grade classroom.
He asked me to sit beside him on
the bed. I hesitated again.
The foam mattress was spotted with holes, as if
someone hungry had taken bites out of it.

And the stench. The smell of urine couldn't
be disguised. But it didn't need to be.
Accidents in the night were common among the teens.
As I sat next to him, I looked around the room.
There were ten other boys, throwing dice on the floor.
And they rocked and rocked. Some sideways, some
back and forth in a robotic and hypnotizing way.
And so quickly, with vacant expressions on their faces.
This was the way they comforted them-
selves as infants in their cribs, unattended.
And this was the way they comforted themselves now.
Just as the small orphaned children I
worked with—it was too familiar.
He sat beside me too, and rocked. His thumb
was in his mouth. It calmed him.
As I looked at the boys around him, I noticed
that their thumbs served as pacifiers too.
I looked into their eyes, but they were not ashamed.
They didn't know they should be.
This was their home; this life was what they knew.
He told me that his back hurt, and that his
back was curved, as he sat hunched,
with his shoulder forward.
I asked him why and he said it kept
him warm to sit this way.
I asked him if he felt cold now. He said he
was fine, as his clothes were layered.
"How many layers?" I asked. "Seven, I
think, so I feel fine," he replied.
The boys were all joking and wrestling with
each other. They would be late for dinner.
But he was really hungry, he told me.
We walked toward the stairwell, and passed a
room full of boys singing praise songs to God.

They sang so loudly. How could they
sing to Him with such passion?
But I knew, it was their only hope.
We walked outside the dining hall.
He held my hand as we walked and I real-
ized I no longer noticed the dirt on his
hands or his stench. What a blessing!
Was it a blessing or would I forget, like he did,
that this is not how a boy should live?
A staff member in the dining hall
yelled again, with such rage.
They had to stand in line quietly as they
waited. And for what? Tea and bread.
He pulled out a broken chair for
me to join him for dinner.
His cheekbones were sharply defined. He was so thin.
He was smaller than he should have been, had
he more to eat in his sixteen years of life.
Tonight he was so hungry. And he ate only bread.
Bread so stale that he had to clench
his jaw just to manage it.
He asked me if I would like some of his
bread. I said, "No, thank you."
I was hungry too, and had an orange in my
jacket to eat later. I hesitated again,
and the shame came over me.
I slid the orange under the table. He hid it in
the pocket of his pants under one of the
many layers that hid his tiny frame.
If someone found it, he would be hit again.
We walked outside and exchanged Romanian
words for English as we looked
upwards. We talked of the sky, the stars, the moon.
I talked of God and he did too, with a smile
so true, I was sure he knew Him.

How could he have such a faith?
My spirit could not rest.
I walked the next day through an apple orchard to find a place to calm my soul.
I sat in the tall grass and a gen-
tle breeze swept across my face.
And the sun soothed me. I knew my spirit
would rest when he left this place he
called home and met his Father, and was held
in His hands, with a new body, pure
and blameless in His sight.

Summer 2001—Age 5

Lukas was playing in his room and he asked, "Mama, how do you know what Hell is like?" I tried in the best way I could to explain this to a five-year-old. Then he said, "When we die, Jesus will tell us." I never had mentioned Hell before so I wondered what made him think of such a subject.

CHAPTER 20

MY NOT SO FAVORITE THINGS

Spring 2002—Age 6

When Lukas was six, we were stuck in traffic on a San Diego highway, and the people in the cars surrounding us were honking their horns. He could see some of them yelling at the driver in front of them. Lukas calmly said, "Don't they know that it's not down here." I asked, "Where?" and he repeated, "Down here. It's with God, not down here." He was telling me that all of this arguing on earth was for nothing, as the real purpose was with God, not with things like traffic "down here on earth."

I went to the market one day and made a point to observe the merchants. Some sold a few eggs and spices, others a handful of potatoes or carrots. One could also find hand-carved wooden spoons or brooms made of straw, but these were the only local crafts I found—things of necessity, but nothing of art for art's sake. The people here did not have money to spare for such things. Their wrinkles seemed to tell me who they were and how they lived their lives. The women wore skirts and scarves called babushkas on their heads, and the men had tall wooly hats. Both women and men stared with steely eyes that recognized that I—with my Eddie Bauer down vest and ski gloves—had not lived as they lived.

I returned to Herculane with the food I had purchased from five different places in town, only to find there was no water. Water was shut off every day, although the time could not be predicted. Warm water was only available for an hour or two every day, although this never seemed to coincide with dishwashing time.

I brought hand wipes from the grocery store in Denver before I came and made a trip to the outhouse. In some of the bathrooms, the toilets couldn't handle the rough toilet paper, so it was thrown in a trash can. I needed to flush the toilet with water I collected from a bucket outside. The trash was then taken to a local spot, two blocks away. I went into the kitchen, and I boiled a pot of water for twenty minutes. No one in this town drank water at any time, as it had so much sediment in it that it was like drinking watery chalk.

Bottled water didn't exist here, so everyone drank soda or tea for meals. It was a good day when the water was running, but that didn't mean it was hot. I needed a shower, so I showered quickly in cold, drizzling water. When I thought back to those merchants, I knew their eyes had seen the truth. My wrinkles would never be the same as theirs.

Iorela asked me if I wanted to join her at the depot for some late evening work. It was already after 8:00 p.m. and we both had worked a full day. I was ready to sit back and read a book or write a letter to a friend, but Iorela seemed to gain energy the later it became. How could I refuse?

We entered the depot that felt more like an igloo, and she explained that Casa Alba had to be stocked with more diapers. I learned that a Swedish diaper company donated defective diapers to the children at Casa Alba. I stared at the mound in front of us that looked like a small mountain with moguls of white fluffy cloth. I thought we would just grab 100 of them, place them in a bag and return to Herculane. Oh, no! We had to sit at the base of the mountain of briefs and wade through them, trying to find diapers that we considered acceptable for the children.

I quickly learned that this was a daunting task. I looked through close to fifty diapers and noticed that either both attachment tabs were missing, or elastic near the legs was exposed and would serve like a tourniquet on their little cherubic legs. Some had the absorbent stuffing was spewing out, which would render the cotton useless. After more than fifteen minutes, I used my hands to shovel my way deeper into the mound and finally discovered one that would meet Iorela's standards. I felt like Willy Wonka after finding the golden ticket! But my excitement was quickly deflated like air whistling out of a popped balloon as I also realized that we would be there for a while.

Iorela and I talked and laughed about inventions we could create to prevent diaper-defects, and we realized that we could at least use duct tape if one or two tabs were missing. I would learn that Jari would gladly volunteer his duct-taping skills whenever asked during diaper duty. We left the depot close to eleven with our bag filled with only enough stock to last a week. I told myself I would never complain when opening up a fresh, new package of Pampers or Huggies once back in the U.S.

CHAPTER 21

THE NIGHT SHIFT

One particular winter evening, I was scheduled for the work shift at night at Casa Alba. Iorela informed me that I was to try to sleep earlier that day as there was lots of work to be done at night. Daytime rest escaped me, so I arrived at the orphanage a bit fatigued. First, I was given a task of sorting and organizing the developmental toys and blocks that were hung in colorful bags, hand-made by the Swedes. After that task was complete, I was responsible for doing the laundry for all twenty-four children, all of whom had inevitably spilled food or drinks on their clothes during the day. I washed and dried at least seven loads of laundry, while one other staff personnel rested in case I was overwhelmed by too many crying children in the night.

Close to two in the morning, after the third load of dirty laundry, I heard a cry that became a shriek. I ran to the dining room area where I found Silvia, Lukas' half-sister, with tears streaming down her cheeks. I should have guessed that it would be Silvia, since the only sound I had ever heard her make were high-pitched shrieks. Desperate to calm her before the other staff person woke up, I lifted her and began singing, but her cries continued. Singing usually calmed children quickly in my experience, but Silvia's cries couldn't be quelled. They actually intensified such that I thought every child would wake from slumber and I would be left with the ensuing pandemonium. She screamed but made sounds that were noxious, and devoid of meaning. Although I held her close and rocked her as I sang, her cries became hysterical. After thirty minutes, my arms were beyond tired since she was a stocky six year old. My voice became hoarse as I sang Christmas carols and songs I remembered from nursery school. I worried that I wouldn't be able to complete my laundry duties and that the staff would think I was a lazy American. After rocking her and singing for one hour, I desperately prayed that God would help me to stop her crying—I was about to burst into tears myself! While I sang Silent Night over and over again, her stiff body began to relax in my arms, her head nestled against my chest, with deep sighs signalling the calm that would follow.

What happened next amazed me. This young girl, who was severely autistic, and who had never made a verbal connection to me or anyone to my knowledge, began to hum to the tune of Silent Night, and with perfect pitch! She then fell asleep in my arms, and I was finally able to tuck her into bed. I was extremely weary, yet thankful to God, and energized to complete the pile of dirty clothes in front of me. The hours of the night shift never seemed as if they would come to an end, and I hoped the same for the memories.

CHAPTER 22

CEAU AMERICANA!

When I worked at Casa Alba, I was able to take Lukas and one or two others for a walk in the stroller. One day, Lukas was dressed in his snowsuit. As we strolled, he looked with such wonder at the birds, roosters and dogs. A little boy named Csaba (pronounced somewhat like chubby) was also along for the ride. We came upon the military practicing war games in an open field below. To see the men wearing green army uniforms while crawling on the ground with their rifles made me feel so vulnerable. The stone wall separating us was broken, and the boys and I could have stepped over the wall and entered their practice battle-field. Images of miniature toy soldiers in a boy's playroom came to mind. I know our military was doing the same thing in the U.S. Yet I didn't want Lukas to see them practicing war, and I swiftly turned around and headed back to Casa Alba.

Interestingly, I walked near to this field alone the next day, and a military man and his young son stopped me and asked where I was from. I said, "America." They were so excited, and they yelled, "Ceau, Americana," or "Hello, Americana" as they walked for the next two blocks. An elderly man overheard this exchange, also greeted me and repeated, "Americana." He then took my hand and kissed it. Everyone I met at the marketplace or at work seemed so excited to meet an American. I think I expected resentment, but I realized that perhaps this war was as far away from their hearts as it was mine.

KRISTI WILKINSON

March 21, 2003—Age 7

Lukas' kindergarten teacher, Miss O'Beirne, asked the students in her class if they'd like to write to the troops individually as the U.S. was at war with Iraq. We were in the car, and he announced he was ready to write his letter. He began so quickly I told him to wait until I could pull off to the side of the road; it wasn't an opportune time to write while I was at the wheel. I luckily found a pen and paper in the car. As he talked, I was able to write his exact words. At age seven, this was what poured out from his heart:

"Dear soldier, I hope you have a safe trip there. Thank you for fighting for our country. You are very brave soldiers. Thank you for protecting America. Don't worry if you die, Jesus always has the stair for you to heaven to live forever. We'll be praying over you and your men that angels are watching over you. Lukas." After he brought the letter to Miss O'Beirne, she and I wondered with a solemn heart which soldier would receive that letter.

CHAPTER 23

A WALK BACK IN TIME

Fall 2000—Age 4

We were driving home from my friend Deborah Simon's house in Evergreen Colorado, and it was close to midnight. Since it was so late at night, I thought Lukas was sleeping. Instead, he asked me, "When do we need new tires?" Since he was a four-year-old, I didn't expect him to be asking me questions about my tires. As a single mom working full-time, I hadn't had much time to take a shower, let alone think of car maintenance. The next day when I inspected the tires, they looked bare. I took my car to the gas station and a feeling of relief swept over me when the mechanic told me they were about to burst and desperately needed to be replaced. Lukas' late night question might have saved us both.

At times I felt so out of place in this village. My appearance, clothing and hairstyle usually gave away the fact that I was not from Marghita. I felt as if I were taken back in time to a different era, perhaps the early 1900s. A few things in Marghita made me imagine life on the prairie or on one of the thirteen new colonies, which I learned about in school. One night while I was working at Casa Alba, I heard the distinct sound of horse hooves clunking down the streets outside and wondered why the horses had come there at that time of night. I peered through the window and learned that the children's dirty diapers were picked up by horse and buggy, and taken miles away to the trash heap.

These buggies and horse-drawn wagons were a common sight throughout the town, and I never lost that urge to sneak out my camera to capture the scene that was unfolding. I would hesitate so that I would not draw attention to myself, or to the persons holding the horse reins. I didn't want to act like this was something out of the ordinary. The same horse-drawn buggies that delivered furniture in this town also collected the trash, and the diapers from Casa Alba. I was thankful that the horses made the pilgrimage to the trash heap, and that I wasn't asked to take the diapers or trash across town by hand-drawn wagon.

One of the duties at Casa Alba was make a trek to the hospital to get the food that was prepared for the children. This sounds like a simple task. It would have been had it not involved those hand-drawn wagons. The worker given this task had to pull two wagons by hand several blocks away to the hospital cafeteria staff who supervised what food was being fed to the children. The Swedes had attempted to take over this responsibility, but the Romanian hospital staff members wanted to keep their hands in this pot. They claimed that the kitchen wasn't adequate at the orphanage.

When my time arrived for this task, I felt like a girl from a storybook in that New England colony, as I walked down the cobblestone street to the hospital, tugging the wagons behind me. I wondered if everyone I passed by would think I looked odd, tugging those wagons. Interestingly, no one expressed the slightest surprise. This was familiar to them. So, I continued down the street until I found the rusty gate that would lead me to the hospital kitchen. The key I was given resembled one fashioned by Abe Lincoln's locksmith, and it actually opened the heavy rusted gate. I found my way to the door that led to the kitchen. I walked up the steps—almost in the dark—and found the women in front of large iron pots, steam streaming past the white caps they wore on their heads. Again, I was reminded of women in colonial days who labored in the kitchens and stirred soup in large pots over an open fire.

Although I knew that those cafeteria ladies saw me, I might as well have been invisible. I had to wait until it was time for the Casa Alba kids to receive their food. I didn't say a word. While I stood waiting in the kitchen, one particular cook startled me. As the woman flung her long, wooden spoon out of a pot of soup, I stared in amazement. Attached to the end of the spoon was a long, greenish sludge, similar to the strands of sea kelp I found on the beach in Southern California! I certainly didn't want to know the ingredients for this soup! As she dangled the "sludge" high above the cauldron, I almost gasped! Could she possibly be trying to impress me with her expert culinary skills? It was hard to contain my laughter until I was back on the street, pulling the wagon with the pots of soup back to the hungry kids at Casa Alba.

On special days, the pots of food we received for the kids may be filled with mashed potatoes or eggs with poppy seeds. Also, a small separate pot was designated for "hepatic," as a few of the kids had hepatitis, and these ladies insisted they should have food without salt. The women made this quite clear with their curt words—the only words spoken to me. As they handed me the five-gallon container of soup, they would say, "Pentru copii mici and copii mare," which meant, "for the small and big children," and then, "Pentru hepatic." I wasn't sure if salt-free food was better for the children with hepatitis, but I surely wouldn't questions these women!

I made my way back to Casa Alba, afraid that I would spill the soup for the "hepatic" before I made it back to the orphanage. This fear came from the fact that the wagons wobbled, and the pots tipped as I pulled it along the street that didn't have a smooth inch on it. I looked inside the pot designated for the "hepatic" and it didn't look like anything more than broth with something indiscernible floating in it. Maybe a cabbage wedge or onion peel. I wasn't quite sure. By the time I made my way back to Casa Alba in ten degree weather, and the children were fed, the food was invariably cold. Needless to say, I wasn't looking forward to my return trip to the kitchen with the wagons and large heavy pots, after I had washed them. I didn't have to imagine what life on the prairie or in the New England colony was like—I felt I was actually living it.

One of the staff members at Casa Alba came to work every day, donning her nursing-type bonnet, and clad in a skirt. I always wondered if the bonnet came off at home—I don't think I'll ever know. She would serve the children food brought from the hospital kitchen, and if that food happened to be potatoes, the mashed spuds would be so solidified, they would lift off of their plates in one big chunk—too large to fit in their tiny mouths. They ate a slice of hard bread with margarine during a typical meal. If this was combined with the the eggs and poppy seeds, their lips and cheeks would be covered with little black seeds. The margarine served as the perfect paste to which the poppy seeds could stick. It was a sight to see!

When driving in or out of Marghita, again I was transported to a different era. There were acres of barren fields that were being farmed in the late winter. I saw one woman wearing a skirt, and a babushka covering her head, throwing seeds by hand that would then make some type of harvest that summer or fall. When I looked out at the fields I was in awe. They continued as far as the eye could see, and yet this one woman was supposed to disperse the seeds on countless acres by hand. It would be a miracle if something grew in this dry land.

On one of my many walks, I also passed two young men who were walking behind their horse, tilling the field by hand. I did hear a tractor of sorts on one farmer's property, but it didn't seem like these two men were so lucky. They would plow and till the land by hand, as was done on the prairie. I truly could not believe that this still occurred, just half the globe away.

Yet another task was to make the main meal that fed all of the volunteers who worked at the orphanages. The number of Swedes to feed could be twenty at one time. This was an all day task. Shopping could take up to two hours, as finding everything needed at one place was rare. One day, when it was my time to make the main meal, Jari asked me, "Will you make tacos?" Because I was from the U.S., it was assumed that I knew how to make tacos. I had made tacos when I was in the states, but when I asked where to find the taco shells, I was told I would have to make them by hand. Also, I could not buy a packet of taco seasoning at the grocery store.

I headed out to the marketplace, and someone mentioned the word paprika. I bought some. Thank God that I asked one of the Swedes about this paprika. It happened to be fifty times as strong as the paprika familiar to me. If I had added it to the meat, I might have been responsible for giving twenty Swedes flaming indigestion. Next, I went to one store for the meat, and one store for the cheese. When I was ready to find something to make the taco shells, I was told I had to find lard. Now lard was not for sale like Crisco or margarine was in the U.S. I had to go to Casa Alba to ask Florica, who was known for her lard, if I could have some of hers. So, I went to her house to get a jar of lard so I could make the shells by hand. As a native of that village, she would have earned meager wages, but she was more than generous with what she had to give.

Then, it was time to find some of the toppings for the tacos. I looked for lettuce and tomatoes, but learned that these could not be found in the winter. I passed one stand at the market, but it was only selling brooms, handmade with straw. No vegetables there. I was running out of time. Next, I had to go to another store for bread, which was served at most meals. When I finished carrying my bags of produce to Herculane, I was exhausted and cold. My hands were raw due to the weight of the bags. More than two hours had transpired, and I had not even begun to cook. To my amazement, after a few more hours in the kitchen, the meal was an unlikely success. Everyone raved over my handmade tacos, thanks to Florica's lard!

CHAPTER 24

TIME WITH THE TEENS

Summer 2000—Age 4

Lukas and I were walking down Humboldt Street in Denver when fire trucks barreled down the road. He had a fascination with fire trucks, but we weren't expecting what we would find. A house near Ninth and Humboldt, bordering Cheesman Park, was in flames. As I stood by that burning house with him on my shoulders he said, "Thank you, God, for giving us a house. I know that Jesus loves me. Hallelujah, Amen." These were the words from the song he sang at mealtimes at Casa Alba. They took on a new meaning as we stood by that house engulfed in flames. We continued to sing that blessing song for over a decade.

I returned to Cadea with Barbro, and when Emeric saw me, he ran to me and jumped into my arms as if he were a young child. Barbro noticed this, and she mentioned that one boy who came to sleep at her apartment brought his stuffed animal, and he was eighteen. One teen sat facing a corner and rocked vigorously as he sang at the top of his lungs. Some boys were coming out of the showers, wearing clothes that were soaking wet.

Then I found a room with boys working on puzzles that Barbro had given to them. One seventeen-year-old, Imre, was struggling with one piece. He seemed so bright. Yet as I watched him, I was amazed to think that he didn't know that a border piece would not fit in the middle of the puzzle. Working with puzzles was something I took for granted and a small thing that represented so much more. Something as simple as child's play would assault his intelligence and perhaps his livelihood at work for the rest of his life. These experiences were the things that drew me to spend time with these boys. I found myself coming to see them at every opportunity I had. I thought I came here to hold babies. Maybe God had people of all ages in mind.

CHAPTER 25

STREET DOGS

It was quite cold outside—maybe twenty degrees—and I prepared to go on another walk. At the last minute, I took my shoes off and exchanged my thin pair of socks for an extra-thick pair of socks that a friend had given to me for the trip. Hoping for refreshment, I dashed out the door before anyone had the chance to stop me with any job requests. The chill certainly was rejuvenating, yet on my return a small dog followed me and seemed to get closer and closer. I quickened my pace, and then suddenly I felt him bite my leg near my ankle. This wasn't the type of refreshment I was looking for, but luckily he backed off and I made it home. Unfortunately, the bite did draw blood, but not much. I realized then, that if I hadn't changed those socks, it would have been much worse. I felt God protecting me with every step.

Unfortunately, I found out from the Swedes that I would need to get a rabies shot. I tried to minimize it, but they insisted. So I made the one hour trip to the hospital in Oradea. When I got there and told them what had happened, they yelled out my plight for the entire waiting room to hear, "Rabies, rabies!" They ushered me toward another room. Before I entered, I looked up at the door frame: on it was posted a sign in bold, black letters, labeled, "Antirabic." Just then they stared at me as if they thought I would start foaming at the mouth, and I quietly entered the room.

After what seemed like a lifetime, a nurse entered the room, wearing a starched white cap. She revealed an extra-long needle that I thought was prepared for my arm. I was disheartened when she swiftly injected it into my abdomen. Finally, I thought I was finished with this ordeal, but the nurse announced that I would need to return for injections for the next seven days. Seven injections! I had no computer access, but I was certain that seven injections wasn't part of the protocol in the states. On day seven, Lars let me borrow one of the cars he often drove for my travel to the hospital in Oradea. While I was driving, I noticed that it was unusually cold inside and that I could feel a strong draft tickling my feet. I quickly looked down and noticed a large hole in the floorboards, the dark road eerily visible below. I gasped to myself at the thought of Lars driving this car without complaint, as he selflessly gave of himself. I figured a small injection was nothing to gripe about! I just hoped the hole didn't grow larger and engulf me along the bumpy road to Oradea.

Once I safely arrived at the hospital, I was assigned a timid new nurse who punctured more than my fatty tissue, and I was left with intense, stabbing pain for the next eight hours. I remember feeling so much pain that I considered returning to the hospital to see if perhaps the nurse had punctured something in my abdomen. Then I realized that the likelihood of getting a clear diagnosis at that hospital was close to nil, so I returned to my evening shift with the children. Later that night, I developed an allergic reaction to the injection and had welts covering my stomach and the lymph nodes in my groin were swollen like small grapes. This was far worse than the dog bite, but I knew one thing for certain—I left that "Antirabic" room without rabies!

October 28, 2003—Age 7

Lukas was at his friend Max Rojas-Domke's house when he ran, tripped and struck his forehead on a coffee table, leaving him with an injury that required stitches. He was starting to panic as the doctor began to stitch up his injury, and so I said a prayer with him. On the way home, he said, "Mom, after the prayer, it was like God put His hand on my forehead and the pain went through His skin first. He was like a shield to me." I shared his description with Max's mom, Parth, that God was His protection during his first trip to urgent care. It brought us both comfort.

CHAPTER 26

HAIR STYLISTS IN TRAINING

O ne evening when I returned to Cadea, I noticed that Attila was giving one of the boys a haircut. I learned that an American woman named Phyllis—also a volunteer through the foundation—was training some of them to become hair-stylists. Most of the boys were gypsies. Because gypsies were usually ostracized from the workplace in this region, Phyllis tried to teach them a skill that they could use. I decided that I should let Attila practice on me and give my hair a trim. I have always had long hair so I thought it would be rather simple for him. I sat in the chair with five other boys watching as he practiced his newly acquired skills on my hair.

After Attila finished, he stood in front of me and then screamed. I was startled to say the least, and wondered what was wrong. He showed me with his hands that one side was about four inches shorter than the other. I burst out laughing. With that frightening scream, I expected to see blood trickling from my neck; the only problem was that I had a half-bob. I responded with a generic, "No problem," and a big smile, and told him to bob the other half. I would be in this town for a while longer, and I don't think the women wearing babushkas at the marketplace would notice.

After my new haircut, Attila revealed a vulnerability that I had not seen before. He explained that he rocked incessantly when he went to bed at night. A disturbing question came next—one that caused the hair on my arms to stand on end. He said, "Do you think I will ever stop rocking? Do you think the rocking will stop when I get married?" My heart ached for this eighteen-year-old. I learned in the book, *A Peacock or a Crow*, about

Romanian orphans, that the seemingly endless, and somewhat furious rocking that I observed in almost all of the children and in the teenagers, could be explained in two ways. Some believed that the rocking was mostly behavioral, and stemmed from the lack of rocking and touch at an early developmental age when it was needed. In essence, those children soothed themselves and rocked themselves to sleep. Other neurologists posed another theory that complemented the first. Some believed that because the children did not achieve the appropriate developmental positions including rolling, crawling, sitting and standing—due to the neglect and confinement to cribs, where they remained in the prone positions for far too long—those children subsequently had equilibrium defects. They therefore needed to rock to stimulate their inner ears and thus their equilibrium system, in order to compensate for the lack of movement that their bodies craved; therefore, by methodically rocking, they could give themselves the necessary input they required to enhance their awareness of their position in space.

No matter which theory was correct—if not a combination of both—I wished there would have been arms to hold these children so that when they were teens, they weren't worried about whether or not their future spouses would find them rocking themselves to sleep.

Attila then inquired about my arrival in his small village. He wondered what led me there. I told him that I felt God guided me to his village, and that He provided everything I needed to come. He told me that he was overwhelmed by feelings of guilt and that he was told he would never go to heaven because he smoked cigarettes.

I told him that none of us would get into heaven if it was based on what we had done in our past. I said that his smoking was like my habit of eating chocolate chip cookies, and that I didn't think that either habit would keep us outside of the heavenly gates. I shared with him about God's forgiveness for every sin, big or small.

I read a Psalm that night stating that if a mother and father would forsake their child, God would not. I felt that God would have been telling Attila that he was not forsaken or forgotten.

May 14, 2003—Age 7

Lukas and I were eating dinner with my Mom and Dad, and he said, "Papa, let's talk about the rooms in heaven." My mom started to chime in and he said, "Nika, this isn't for you, these questions are for Papa." So he started again with his questions for Papa, and he said, "How many rooms do you think there are? Do you think everyone will have their own room? Do you think the rooms will be two story (or one on top of another), like a house here? Do you think everyone will find their room?" His questions went on and on. I am not sure if he knew that at the time, my Dad did not believe in heaven. He seemed certain that these questions were for Papa. My mom and I sat silently as they discussed heaven's rooms.

CHAPTER 27

VISIT FROM VICTORIA

I mentioned that I met a girl named Victoria in Budapest before arriving in Romania, due to the man who was sitting next to me on the plane from New York to Budapest. I felt an urge to call Victoria, and after many failed attempts, I got in touch with her. Remember, there were no cell phones or answering machines. Then she decided to come the next day, and took the four-hour train ride to Oradea. I met her, along with a teenager from the Cadea orphanage named Onti. He helped lead me to the train station and to the track where she would be. We slept that night for only five hours, and then I brought her to Casa Alba, where we played with the children most of the day. We took Lukas, Gusztav, and Csaba for a two-hour walk through the back-streets of Marghita, lifting them up to see chickens in people's yards, and stopping each time they wanted to stop to pick up a rock or a stick. I told her how much I loved Lukas and that even though I was not supposed to have favorites, that he had stolen my heart!

After we left Casa Alba, I had a chance to rest while Victoria visited a nearby orphanage named Popesti for middle school aged children. An hour later, we went to Cadea so that she could meet the teenage boys at that orphanage. I played soccer—a Romanian favorite—with Emeric and two other boys named Kolomon and Bogdan, during which they showed me their true passion for the game. Even though I am female, they also showed me no mercy. While I played soccer, Victoria talked with Attila and a boy named Mickey. When I joined her, I could see the joy she had while communicating in limited Romanian. We went inside with Attila and found a boy named Karcsi, and the two of them sang the most beautiful song to us. Meanwhile, Emeric sat next to me, listening as well. They were singing a worship song to God and it felt as if God were in the room with us. Victoria asked if we could pray. All of us held hands and prayed a prayer in simple Romanian that seemed just as broken as these teens. The prayer seemed to rise, lifting our spirits at the same time.

September 28, 2002—Age 6

My friend Erica Viviani, Lukas and I went back to Colorado for a visit, and she took me to see a friend who was battling cancer. It had spread throughout her body to her brain. Before we left, we said a prayer together. I sat with her, holding Lukas on my lap as he cradled his camel in his hands. He was so quiet, I thought he was sleeping, but as we sat in silence for a moment, Lukas said, "God, baptize her with your love." I had never thought of baptism as being an outpouring of love, but we both were blessed by his prayer.

Victoria and I reflected on the day spending time with children from three different orphanages. She talked to me about Emeric's room, with the bed that was really a metal cot with a thin mattress, saturated in urine. We talked about the broken windows at Cadea that let in the zero-degree air, so that I could see my breath as if I were outside. We spent about seven hours with them, and agreed that these hours made up one of the most memorable and poignant days of our lives. She returned to Budapest, and told me that this experience had changed her forever.

CHAPTER 28

WELCOME NEW BABIES

Summer 2000—Age 4

I sang to Lukas before he went to sleep every night and I always ended with the song "Amazing Grace." One night, I quieted my voice and I heard him singing the words, "Amazing grapes how sweet and sour." Oh, how I didn't realize that he thought I was singing about sweet and sour grapes every night.

A big day arrived at Casa Alba when twin sisters Ottilia and Ibolya—two of the cutest babies I have ever seen—were welcomed to live there. They had ringlet curls and dimples that deepened when their smiles beamed, somewhat reminiscent of Shirley Temple. I was going to get the chance to care for them for a week, just before another newborn named Gizelle would come. At that time, Casa Alba did not have more than two children under aged two, so having three new babies would add a new dimension to the child care. All of the Romanian workers, as well as the Swedes, were overwhelmed with compassion for these girls, and for all the new babies that arrived.

As I spent almost every day at Casa Alba taking care of Lukas, he became jealous when I would hold the babies, and would cry so loudly that I would inherently feel the need to hold him instead. I had little time for physical therapy exercises, but if Lukas was entertained by playing with Gusztav, I would work with a little girl named Lavinia who needed strengthening for her delayed body. She was two, but could hardly sit, and was unable to stand or take steps while holding on to something or someone—what some babies can do at nine months. She was emotionally detached as well, and would stare off into a distant unknown place. Even though I had limited time with her, I could see changes in her tiny torso and hoped I would get to see her stand before I returned home to Denver.

The kids at Casa Alba were napping, and I had time to talk to one of the wonderful caregivers named Ligia who was from that village. She was especially fond of Lukas and spent as much time with him as she could when she was assigned to his room. Not only did she care for him during the day, but at times, she would invite him into her family's home for a night, not as a job, but out of love for him. I asked her about adoption at Casa Alba, and if she was interested in adopting Lukas. I privately wanted to inquire for myself, but didn't want to seem like a presumptuous American since I had only been there a few months. She replied, "Single women are not encouraged to adopt children in Romania. That is the custom here."

I was heartbroken for her—as I knew she adored him—and also for myself since I was single. That dashed my hopes of possibly adopting him someday. Knowing that she lived with her family, I asked if her family could adopt him and she could care for him. She said that they could not afford to adopt and wished they could, but they couldn't. Then she mentioned that international adoptions were about $15,000, or so she had heard. Well, that would count me out. I was volunteering here, and I only had about $700 in the bank, as I was still paying off student loans. I resolved myself to praying for him to find the perfect home and family to call his own.

I talked to Iorela about adoptions and why the children were not being adopted from Casa Alba. She explained that all of the children at the orphanage were stuck in the system, so to speak, as they were not declared abandoned. I asked her why and she replied, "This village is so small and far from any city that it has no social worker. The social worker is needed to facilitate the adoption process, and to legally declare the children abandoned. It takes six months for them to be declared abandoned. In that time, if the family returns to visit the child, or takes them home for a few days and then wishes to return them to the orphanage, the six-month process begins again."

I couldn't believe this. No social worker could be found in this village. But then when I surveyed the town in my mind, I could believe this. The children were then trapped unless a social worker was found. I asked Iorela if they were looking for a social worker—thinking to myself that I hoped the process would someday start for Lukas—and she affirmed to me that she and Lars were trying to find one from Oradea, a city about one hour away. She had an interest in this too, as she had an incredible bond with Gusztav, and had expressed her interest in providing him with a home. I realized that the wheels turned slowly in this village.

CHAPTER 29

THE DISCIPLINE OF LISTENING

January 28, 2007—Age 11

Lukas and I had just learned that our worship leader at church had suffered a terrible loss. His brother-in-law died unexpectedly, leaving behind four young children. We were both asking questions about death and other topics. Then Lukas said, "Mom, I am getting a thought that God is telling me. It is hard to understand when someone dies. It is not to be foretold in the present, it is to be foretold in the future." I don't think Lukas ever used the word foretold. Because he didn't generally read books unless I read them to him due to his dyslexia, I knew he had not come upon this word while reading. I asked him again about this and he repeated, "The thought is something God is telling me that we will not understand now." He then added, "I really don't understand what it means, but it is for all people." Then he said, "If I ever write about all the things God has told me, I'll name the book just that, 'The things God has told me' or maybe I'll call it, 'The child who listens.'" I wondered about the words, "It is not to be foretold in the present." I wondered if he meant that we wouldn't get the answers about death here on earth. We would have to wait for these answers. I wasn't sure (and Lukas wasn't either), but he wanted his words to be for all people.

After work that day, I went for my ritualistic hillside walk. Barbro had asked me to speak at the worship service that night, and I was thinking of talking about trust or thirsting after God. I asked God to guide me in my words for that night. I decided to sit on the hillside overlooking Marghita, and as I sat in silence, I realized how many sounds I hadn't noticed while my thoughts clouded my mind on this same path a few steps away. Sitting by an abandoned house, I heard the sound of sheep, a cow, two different birds, dogs, a horse, and even a mouse. Just then I realized that God was trying to get me to listen to Him, just listen. He wanted me to learn how to hear Him when He was trying to speak to me.

I returned to Herculane and hibernated in my bunk to look for verses from the Psalms about hearing His voice, and happened upon Psalm 29. The Hebrew words of the Psalm say, "The voice of the Lord is upon the waters, the glory of the Lord thunders…The voice of the Lord is powerful and majestic. The voice of the Lord breaks the cedars." These words spoke to me and reminded me that His voice can be heard around me and in nature if I would just take a minute to slow down and listen.

I was busy trying to "hear" God when a girl named Gabriella came into the bunk room, and startled my solitary state with words of the street children in the city who sniffed glue. I hoped she couldn't tell I was listening to her half-heartedly. Instead of giving her my undivided attention, I kept looking down to scroll for verses. Then I realized I had to stop and listen to her. She then said to me, "God spoke to my heart and told me to tell you not to give up or stop with the work here, and to keep following Him." In my busyness preparing the study on listening, I almost missed her message, and His message as well. God can say so much more when we are silent.

Another of my daily walks reinforced this humbling lesson. I was walking alone, enjoying my solitary time, when I crossed a bridge and saw an older man fishing. I said "Ceau," or "Hello" to be friendly, but not necessarily as an invite for him to join me. When he put down his rod to walk along with me, I was rather startled. I thought he might follow me for several yards, and return to his rod, but he remained with me for the next fifteen minutes. I struggled with phrases and he rambled as if I understood everything he said. He insisted that I join him for coffee. After trying to dissuade him once, I felt drawn to accept his offer.

Somehow we were able to understand the main themes of our conversation. When he asked me why I came to this village, I told him that I felt God led me here to work with the children. He then confided in me his private and personal struggle with alcohol and how it seemed to depress and imprison him. I was able to tell him that I would pray that God would break his merciless bond with alcohol and lift him from the cycle of guilt it brought.

As we left the smoky restaurant, the sun was setting and the sky was stained with a fiery red that seemed to burn for him. He smiled as we said goodbye, and as I walked along the broken and unused train tracks, I thanked God for the unexpected time with this man—his simple offer I had at first turned down.

June 7, 2005—Age 9

Lukas and I were sitting in my car facing a tree with a broken branch that looked reattached and supported by a metal bar. Lukas said to me, "Do you see the tree, Mama? I have a thought about this tree. It reminds me of the person who has fallen away from God. He is like that branch. But he realizes he needs to be put back on the tree because the tree is God and he needs to be with God. But the metal support will always remind him of what it was like to be away from the tree and from God. So now he knows he has to be with the tree, he needs to be attached to the tree because the tree is God." I have to admit that when I first saw the tree, I just saw a tree with a broken branch. I never looked at a tree with a broken branch the same way again.

CHAPTER 30

BAKING WITH THE BOYS

August 28th, 2002—Age 6

Lukas and I were in the kitchen mixing dough to make gin-gerbread men and he asked me to find the cookie cutter in the shape of a gingerbread man. I said it would be much more fun to make them from our hands. At first he thought that it would be too difficult that way. After thinking for a moment, he said, "Let's make them with our hands. Then we can see how hard it was for God to make us." We continued to make our gingerbread men by hand. With each one, Lukas reminded me of God's handiwork on earth.

I promised a few of the Cadea boys—Attila, Karcsi, and, of course, Emeric—that they could come to Herculane to eat lunch and then make chocolate chip cookies. This was something I had done hundreds of times, but something they had never done. There were no chocolate chips in Marghita. This came as a shock to me since there are so many different types in the States, including milk, semi-sweet and 60 percent dark chocolate, to name just a few. So I had to buy Romanian chocolate bars to improvise.

The boys started to measure the flour, and they had such determined spirits. Emeric was in charge of measuring the sugar, and he proceeded in spilling the entire container of sugar onto the floor, and was overcome with disappointment. I decided that he should look for measuring spoons instead, and he found a can opener. He said he had never seen one, and I was reminded of the things I took for granted growing up with a family. Attila was trying to brush up on his English, and Karcsi was trying to learn how to cut chocolate into small chunks. At one time, all three of them were calling my name: "Kristi, Kristi, Kristi," reminding me of the young children at Casa Alba. Emeric asked me to make sure his apron was a little tighter, and beamed as it draped over his small frame.

When we finished and they tasted the cookies, Emeric asked if he could come back to bake cookies every day. Two days later, I came home from Casa Alba to find Emeric waiting at the Herculane gate. It had taken him a few hours to travel from Cadea and then he waited for me for a few more so that we could bake again. I had no idea that he would be there. I was so happy to see him, but sad at the same time. I was happy that he had come to spend time with me. I knew that his smile masked his broken spirit, and matched the crooked cartwheel he used to greet me. But I was saddened at the thought that I could not give him everything that he needed. It was already March, and I would be returning to the States that month. That meant I would no longer be able to spend even a minute with him, let alone a few hours baking cookies. My limited time with him only scratched the surface of his true needs.

July 12th, 2001—Age 5

After we had moved to San Diego, Lukas and I were on our way to Poway Lake when he announced, "I want a daddy. When am I going to get a daddy? Is he already on earth? Is God going to send him from heaven?" After I tried my best to answer these questions and tell him that I didn't know whether or not he would get a daddy, he said, "If I don't get a daddy on earth, God is the best daddy in the universe."

CHAPTER 31

LEARNED SILENCE

Just before I returned to the U.S., I was able to go to the hospital where the orphaned babies were—the ones who were placed in an official orphanage. Iorela asked me to join her as we brought Gizelle—only nine days old—to Casa Alba. I stared through a glass window at eight more babies lying in metal cribs that were covered with chipped white paint and patches of rust. They seemed imprisoned by these white metal bars. And the room had such a pungent smell. I cannot describe what it felt like to look at the scrawny babies with big brown eyes, yet lying still without a tear and without emotion, with vacant expressions on their faces. Caregivers placed cloth diapers on them that were bound so tightly that they became like straight-jackets for the lower torso. This technique—which included a tight knot tied near their bellies—would restrict their movement so they were confined to their backs. They couldn't roll side to side or try to sit up and thus their development was grossly stunted.

One would think this was reprehensible, yet the caregivers did not want the babies to crawl out of their cribs and hurt themselves—they had limited number of caregivers for each child. Sometimes one for twelve. At other orphanages it was reported there could be one caregiver for up to 100 children. The babies also learned not to cry, since no one would respond even if they cried. The caregivers would actually scold the Swedish volunteers at first if they tried to pick up the babies to comfort them, as this would encourage crying. If the caregivers were vigilant about refusing to pick the babies up, they would again become silent. I was so thankful to be bringing Giselle out of this place at such a young age, where she would be held whenever she needed affection. At the same time, it was painful to leave the room with the others left behind. I thought the other kids at Casa Alba, and of Lukas, lying in this room as infants without being held. I was never more thankful for Lars and Barbro and the selfless work they had begun in this small town.

August 25, 2003—Age 7

Lukas asked me, "What's Satan like?" I wasn't quite sure how I'd explain his character but I said, "I think he's like a fake God." He waited a little while as he thought about my response and then replied, "No, Mom. He's not like a God, he's like the Lord of death."

CHAPTER 32

PREPARING TO SAY GOODBYE

My last day in Maghita was approaching so I went to Cadea for the last time to see the boys. After we visited, Emeric walked me to the car as he played the harmonica. He had a grin that enhanced his dimples that were so deep they held stories of their own. Moments later, Attila, who had given me the haircut, told me that he had a dream that my mom and I returned to Romania the night he prayed for us to return. A few of the boys gave me flowers as it was close to women's day in Romania. A seventeen-year-old named Kolomon drew me a picture of a sun that was smiling, and birds and a cross. It looked so elementary, but was precious to me. He asked for the picture just before I left so that he could make final touches of improvement—another priceless gesture. Another teen named Zoli, who had spent most of his life in the orphanage, also came to say goodbye. He had endured so much, but was planning on going to a university and had so much drive and passion, despite his past experiences. I was amazed at the work that the Swedes had done for him and for these young teens.

It was the third of March and I was to leave in a few days. Iorela told me of journals and photo memory books made for each child at Casa Alba in which the caregivers could capture special moments. These books would then be given to the kids if they were to find homes, or when they were old enough to receive them. I was the first one to write in Lukas' journal. I commented on how excitedly he greeted the children from the "yellow room," especially Gusztav, if he hadn't seen them for a few hours. He hugged and kissed his "brothers" as if he hadn't seen them in weeks. I was glad that I was able to leave my impressions in a book that he would take with him after he left Casa Alba.

I had become friends with many of the Romanian caregivers while I was there, including Monica, Ligia and Tina. I admired them for the passion they had for the children. I could see the tender care that they gave, just as they would give to their own. Monica would often take a little girl named Imelda to her home, or on walks. Although Imelda had developmental delays and was mostly non-verbal, she had such a beautiful bond with Monica, one that was visible without words. This may have been unusual as they treated the gypsy children with the same care as they would a Romanian child. And in this village, I was pretty sure this was not a typical practice. They looked beyond class lines and for this I was so grateful.

One of the Romanian workers who had amazed me with potty-training skills, Inci, invited me into her home for a meal before I departed. We had become good friends while we cared for the toddlers together. She was so gracious, and prepared a tasty meal for me, using the meager wages that she received. Reflecting on what I had learned from Lars, that she may have lived on fifty dollars a month, the three course meal meant that much more to me.

My last day of work at Casa Alba arrived. My group of four children were playing. Luckily, I had time with Lavinia, with her weakened frame and jet black hair. I held her up on her two feet and let go, and she stood for eight seconds—something amazing to see when some thought she would never walk! Maybe someday I would get to see her taking steps. But this was a gift enough for me to witness. After seeing Lukas and Gusztav almost every day for three months, I couldn't imagine saying goodbye, not knowing if I would ever see them again. They were playing outside in a sandbox. They stood in their puffy snowsuits, unaware that "Kitty" wouldn't be here after today. I gave them both a hug and said I would be going back to America, something I knew they could not comprehend. My eyes filled with tears. I didn't want to upset them, so I didn't let the flood come until I closed the gate at Casa Alba, and walked away.

The Swedes then hosted a goodbye party for me at Barbro and Lars' apartment. Although the party was for me, I was greeted by at least five teenagers who slept on their apartment floor since they did not have a bed or a home of their own. They had a feast for me of tomatoes, cheese, cucumbers and handmade bread—the Swedes have a gift for making bread. I was so honored that they would do this for me. They gave me a cookbook filled with Swedish recipes, made by Carina, and deciliter measuring cups so I could follow the recipes back in the States. We spent so much time baking and cooking together in the kitchen to prepare meals for up to twenty volunteers. Sometimes we spent time cooking or baking to escape the reality of this place. This gift would have a deeper meaning for me than any other recipe book.

It was time to board the train from Oradea to Budapest, and a few of the Swedes who drove me there were ready to say goodbye. I gave my last hugs to Henrika and Frida, and Henrika handed me a card to read on the train. I was so grateful that an older man wanted to help me with my bags, thinking how thoughtful he was. He came and sat in the same train car with me. I waved to them as the train pulled away, and just before I was about to sit down, the man started to talk to me. He got close as if to hug me, and I thought he was acting like a concerned grandpa until he took hold of my vest and pulled me toward him and tried to kiss me. I pushed him away and told him, "No," but he still settled into my train car.

I started to read my Bible, thinking that this was a book many would recognize, hoping it would deter him. When a woman with a pink wool coat stepped out of our car to smoke, he touched my leg and kept trying to inch closer to me. But I took hold of his left hand and touched his wedding band on his ring finger, to send a message. Silently, I said a prayer that I would not be alone on this train with him for hours. Minutes later, a woman with a starched shirt, gloves to her forearms, and a stern appearance—like a head librarian—entered our car and sat next to him. I continued to read the Psalms, and thank God, he kept his hands to himself!

A moment came to read the card given to me by Henrika. In it was a handmade card of brown construction paper with a picture of Lukas on it, with a pouty expression and dried tears in his eyes. I cried inside and tears threatened to spill out, but I contained them for fear that the man may feel I needed to be comforted.

Victoria, who had visited me in Marghita, was at the Nyugati train station in Budapest to greet me, with a smile and a tulip—a refreshing welcome after that train ride. When she was visiting me in Romania, she had the idea that I should stay with her for a few days in Budapest before heading back to the U.S. to ease the transition back home. I was grateful for the time to share my experiences with her, and to explore the beautiful city of Budapest. While she worked for the next two days, I walked up and down the streets, discovered forts and castles, found the "Buda," and the "Pest" side of the city, never knowing that the two names were combined to make that fine city. I took photographs of the wonderful bridge that joined the "Buda" to the "Pest" side, as well as statues, colorful homes and churches, and of fine architecture that was so different from the familiar American style. Although sad to say goodbye to Victoria and that incredible city, I was ready to return home.

CHAPTER 33

HOME SWEET HOME

May 10, 2003—Age 7

Billy Graham was going to be speaking in San Diego, and I told Lukas a little bit about him. He then said, "I need to go and see this man. I think He has talked to more people about God than anyone other than Moses, so I need to go and see him." He then said to my dad, "Papa, you need to come with me too." I hadn't mentioned Moses or how many people he had talked to, but he seemed to have a sense of this man for his young age.

As I flew home to the U.S., I tried to prepare myself for the waves of culture shock. I felt guilty that I could buy any type of fruit or vegetable, fifty different types of cereal and a pint of Ben and Jerry's at any of five different stores within ten minutes of my house. I walked down Sixth Avenue near Cherry Creek, with two-story historic brick homes that seemed like palaces, and people walking Golden Retrievers and Labradors—a far cry from the street dogs that roamed the streets in Marghita. Although I enjoyed the comforts and charm of my apartment on Humboldt Street near Cheesman Park, a part of me wanted to jump on a plane and return to Marghita. The photo of teary-eyed Lukas sat on my bedside table as a reminder of him and the other children that I dearly missed. I hoped it would also serve as a reminder of the pleasures I was able to experience every day at home. When I looked at the photo every morning and night, I said a prayer for him and the other children.

A day or two after my return, a friend of mine named Bill said to me, "Kristi, there is a house close to downtown that I want you to see. You are single, and I think it would be a good investment for you to buy a house. I could help you fix it up. I think you should come and see it."

I replied, "I just stepped off of the plane. I haven't made a dime in three months, and I only have $700 in the bank. That's not enough to buy a couch, let alone a house."

He insisted, suggesting that he would help me find and manage renters, and do the remodeling work. For this help, we could split the profit when we sold it someday. He wanted to look at it right away, so although I was still recovering from jet lag, I agreed to take a look. It was a cold rainy night, and I got out of his jeep and stood across the street from the small Victorian house near Seventeenth Street. Something drew my attention to a church just down the street. As I looked at the steeple, with a mist brushing my cheeks, it was as if I heard the words, "This house could bring you the money you need to adopt Lukas someday."

Without hesitation, I met with a real estate agent the next day. I found out that the house was a HUD home, and that there was a special program to entice first time home-owners to buy homes for one percent of the price. I asked the realtor what the price was. She said, "The house is selling for $70,000, so you could buy it with a $700 dollars down payment."

I almost fainted! Since that was the exact amount I had in the bank, I decided to buy it without even going inside. It was March 24, which just so happened to be my birthday, and I thought this was the best birthday present I could give myself. I found out a week later that the house was mine. The agent remarked that she had never completed a closing in only seven days, but that mine would be her first. I didn't know what the future held, but this decision gave me excitement for what could be ahead.

There was a logical side of me that wondered what options I had to come up with the money to adopt Lukas, if that ever became a possibility. I had a friend named Ryan who worked at a bank in Denver, and I boldly asked him if I would be able to get a loan for $15,000. He knew that I had just returned from Romania and also that I was interested in adopting Lukas; he was also aware of the cost. He answered with disappointment in his voice, "No, Kristi, you wouldn't qualify for that amount of a loan. Not with student loans and also little to no savings."

I appreciated his honesty but felt a deep ache in my heart. At the same time, I realized that I would need to walk forward and listen to what I felt God was guiding me to do. The one thing I knew for sure was that I wanted to return to Romania. I couldn't guess where my path would lead me, but I would return to see Lukas and the children I loved in that corner of the world.

July 27, 2003—Age 7

Lukas went to watch a karate class with his neighbor Daniel to see whether or not karate was something he wanted to pursue. He watched a class and saw all of the students bowing to the master instructor. As we left, I asked him what he thought about the class and he said, "I'm not sure about karate, Mom." I asked why, and he replied, "I won't bow to anyone except my God."

CHAPTER 34

BACK TO WORK

I returned to work at Spalding Rehab Hospital, and found it interesting that several of my patients started talking to me about adoption. Some talked about how they wished they had adopted, and some just asked me if I had thought about adopting any of the children there. I thought again about Lukas, and I responded that I hoped he would find that special family.

Three co-workers named Joan Eckrich, Karen Hookstadt and Camma Love—all occupational therapists that I worked with—asked why I couldn't bring a child home. They didn't know about the restrictions in the paperwork, the costliness of the adoptions, and that there wasn't even a social worker in Marghita to declare any of the children abandoned. Thus, none of them were yet eligible for adoption. I explained also that single women couldn't adopt in Romania, so I was out of luck unless I met my husband sometime soon.

A month later, I was assigned to be a clinical instructor for a physical therapy student, named Kristi Dmytriw. She was dynamic and intelligent, a born leader, and also strong in her faith like me. Near the end of her affiliation at Spalding, I invited her to my house, along with a few other friends and co-workers who wanted to see photos I had taken as slides while in Romania. She was still studying intensely and couldn't work at the time, but insisted in giving me money that I could send to help the orphans at Casa Alba. I had made an arrangement with Lars, the foundation director and "father Christmas" in Marghita, to get funds directly to him and the children if I received any money in the States.

A few weeks later, after Kristi had already successfully completed her student affiliation at Spalding, she called me and her voice was full of excitement. She said, "Kristi, you are never going to believe who I met!" Her excitement was palpable as she began to tell me the first part of the story. While she was driving towards her house in Arvada, she felt a strong message to pull over into the parking lot and stop into the hair salon. She had passed the hair salon before, but had never gotten her hair cut there. Although she wasn't in dire need of a haircut, she felt an urgency to go inside. Immediately she was greeted by a nice woman who offered to cut her hair. Kristi had just seen the slides at my apartment of all of the children, and she began to tell the woman about her work with me at Spalding and my experiences in Romania.

Well, the woman replied, "Oh, how interesting. I also worked in Romania, in an orphanage in a small village." Kristi asked her the name of the orphanage and the woman replied, "Casa Alba." Kristi was almost sure that this was the same orphanage where I had worked. So she called me to see if we had worked at the same place.

I said to Kristi, "Was the woman's name Phyllis?"

She said, "Yes, how did you know?" I obviously hadn't told her any details of my lopsided haircut while in Romania.

I couldn't believe it! I had told her that the teenagers at Cadea wanted me to find this lady named "Phyllis" once I returned to Denver. While in Romania, I told the teens—with a chuckle that reflected their ignorance—that it would be close to impossible for me to find her. Since I didn't know where she worked or even her last name, I explained to them that it would be close to impossible to find her. It was hard for them to imagine this as they lived in a small village where they could find just about anyone with a simple description. Yet in a city with more than one million people, it would be hard for me to call every salon to find a lady named Phyllis. They insisted that I had to find Phyllis and come back to Romania with her someday, and they prayed that I would find her. Well now, it looked as though my student, Kristi and her trip to the hair salon would lead me to

Phyllis. I somehow knew then that I would travel to Romania with Phyllis. Their prayers had been answered.

I got Phyllis' phone number from Kristi, and we connected and shared stories about the teenagers and children at Casa Alba. A few months later, Phyllis called me to tell me that there was a cheap flight to Budapest. On October 23, 1998, we were boarding a plane together to fly to Marghita, to work with children we loved.

September 4, 2003—Age 7

Lukas was talking about God and he described him like this, "He's bigger than infinite—ten times infinite, infinite and beyond: He's bigger than all of the numbers and letters built up on each other, one, two, three—and higher and higher. He's so big we can't believe it. We're littler than ants to Him. How can we say anything to Him because He's so loud we can't hear Him the way we talk to each other. It would be like a big sound shock if he talked . . . like big voice cords, boom, boom, boom, boom." I was surprised that a seven-year-old could conceptualize God in infinite terms.

CHAPTER 35

SWEET REUNION

April 15, 2005—Age 9

Lukas was getting ready for bed and he said to me, "I don't know how I could love you more. The only way I know how is to look to Jesus' path to love you more." I thought this was a beautiful way for him to tell me how much he loved me.

As soon as I stepped foot in Marghita, I could hardly wait to go to Casa Alba and reunite with Lukas. Since Lukas was not yet three years old, and I hadn't seen him in over seven months, I was almost sure that he would not recognize me. I prepared my heart for this. When I entered the hallway that led to the room where he was playing, he dropped his toy and ran down the hall into my arms. Of course I cried, but I turned my head so that he wouldn't notice my tears. Iorela informed me that the documents still weren't processed that would allow him to be adopted, but I continued to dream that one day this would be possible.

Phyllis and I stayed in Marghita for almost a month, working with the children at Casa Alba by day, and driving thirty minutes to Cadea in the evenings to spend time with the teenagers.

One evening I met with a teen named Attila, who had been praying that I would return with Phyllis. He smiled from ear to ear, and said with confidence, "I knew you both would come, I just knew!" I admired his confident faith and was humbled by the lack of mine. I marveled at his skills as I watched Phyllis teach him and a few others new haircutting techniques. Soon, the Swedes were going to open a salon where the teens could work, in a town where they typically could not, due to the burden they carried as "gypsies."

Iorela placed me on the working schedule with the same children from the "yellow room" during my days in Marghita. One night I recall as vividly as if it happened yesterday: I was on night duty, which began at ten in the evening and ended at seven in the morning. As the children went to bed at eight o'clock, none of them knew who was working that night. It was about three in the morning, and I had just finished four loads of laundry. I was quietly walking down the hall to put the clothes in the children's cabinets and Lukas called out, "Kitty, Kitty." I was surprised that out of twenty personnel, he recognized me by the sound of my footsteps. I went into his room and he said in Romanian, "Lift me up, Lift me up to the window."

I wondered why he wanted to be lifted up to the window at three in the morning, but I didn't ask why. He said, "Lift me up to the window so I can kiss the wind." I thought this was a profound request for a three-year-old. I wondered if he wanted the wind to kiss him as he didn't have a parent to do so.

Although this trip lasted only one month, I savored each moment I spent with Lukas and also with the teens at Cadea. After work each day at Casa Alba, I went to Cadea to be with the teens. During my first trip, I had written a letter to my friend Heather Neely in San Francisco, describing how the teens often showered wearing their clothes, as this was the only means they had to wash those clothes. Most of them only had one pair of underwear. This image horrified her, and prior to the trip, she sent me packages of clean underwear to take to the teens at Cadea. When I arrived with my bundle, it was as if I had the most prized possession. To them, I am sure it was. Sadly, most of the teens that I knew from the U.S. took basic items like these for granted.

After returning from time with the teens at Cadea, I also had the chance to spend more time talking with a boy named Zoli. He had lived at Cadea, and once he had completed high school, he was no longer allowed to live there. If it had not have been for the support of the foundation, he would have been homeless. Barbo Gustavsson and a girl named Cicci

Axelsson—both from Sweden—took him and about twelve other boys to live in the Black Forest of Transylvania, known as Padurea Neagra. They all lived in a large, two-story building that was owned by the hospital in Marghita, but was rented by the foundation for ten years. It was renovated to provide housing for the teen-aged male orphans for the winter and summer camps for the orphans. Barbro and Cicci served as parents for the teens and trained them in everything from cooking to hygiene. I had visited them a few times, and always remember that I felt warmer outside than inside their "home" on a zero degree day. It is safe to say that the building had no heat. I learned of Zoli's aspirations to continue with his education and one day adopt a child. Even though he was only eighteen and didn't have a mother or father, and had endured many hardships and abuses in the orphanage, I was struck with admiration that he wanted to provide this love to a child. This astounded me especially since he hadn't had the blessing himself. He was only one of the countless teens that had "aged" out of the orphanage system. If it weren't for Barbro and Lars, the many Swedish volunteers, and the Romanians in town that gave of themselves to care for these boys, I shuddered at the thought of their future that seemed destined for failure.

CHAPTER 36

Bonds So Strong

October 20, 2005—Age 9

I was chosen as Mom of the Month at his school, which really meant that out of the many moms who volunteered at his school, my name was the lucky one to be drawn from the hat. Lukas had to introduce me in front of the whole school and he was a bit disappointed that I didn't give a speech; instead I just thanked the school for picking me. That night I said to him, "I couldn't be Mom of the Month without you as my son." He replied, "And without me, you would have been in your old house with just a memory of the boy who wanted to be with you." After this remark, I was never more grateful for being a mom.

It was time to say goodbye to Lukas again, not knowing if I would ever see him again. This goodbye was more difficult for me, perhaps because of the little time I had to spend with him, and perhaps because I knew that he was getting closer to eligibility for adoption. Nonetheless, I hugged him as if it might be my last, and saved the tears until I was beyond the Casa Alba gates.

I returned to the U.S., and received a cassette tape from Iorela. It had praise music from groups like Hillsongs United, and on it Iorela wrote the words that she would ask Lukas. She would ask, "Unde Kristi?" or "Where is Kristi?" and his reply was, "In Amelika" (his pronunciation of America). I thought of him every time I listened to the music on that tape.

One day, while driving East on Fourteenth Street, I listened to a song that I had heard for the first time in Romania called "Bonded Together." While I was singing the song, I started thinking of Lukas and of how strong a bond I felt with him, and was overwhelmed with tears. Just then, I looked up and noticed the car in front of me. I was amazed that the license plate read, "Kitty," the name Lukas called me because he couldn't pronounce my name Kristi with the "r" sound. Some may say it was mere coincidence; but I felt that although we were many miles away, he was close to me in spirit. This moment rekindled my desire to adopt Lukas and bring him home to Colorado with me one day.

A few months later, at the end of January 1999, I went to a concert in Boulder, CO, with my friend Sandi Dollar from the University of Richmond. In the middle of the concert, I started thinking and dreaming about what it would be like to adopt Lukas. At that moment, I focused on the lyrics to the song, "The Wishing Tree." I must mention that at the time, I was thirty-one and Lukas was three. The woman singing the song said, "I was sitting below the wishing tree, wishing for you when I was thirty-one and you were three." Again, I was overwhelmed by the words that rang so true in my heart. I have never been an overly emotional girl prone to crying, but I couldn't contain myself and felt my eyes filling with tears again. Sandi wondered why I was in tears, and I explained to her what I felt when I heard the lyrics of the song and the connection I felt with Lukas. I think then we both understood that I longed to have him as my son.

CHAPTER 37

IORELA'S DIVINE INTERVENTION

August 2008—Age 12

Lukas went to a church service in Oregon and he said, "Mom, the sermon was frustrating to me." I asked him why, and he said, "The minister just talked about facts, facts, facts—facts that would prove that God and Jesus existed. The thing is, Mom, people can hear all of the facts in the world. It's not about facts. It's about faith. Without faith, they still won't believe."

Midway through the winter, I got a message from Iorela that made the hairs on the back of my neck stand still. She told me that Lukas and Silvia's mother had come to Casa Alba to talk to Iorela and that she wanted to take her two children back to her home. Iorela told her that it wouldn't be in the children's best interest to take them at that moment. She recommended that she should return to Casa Alba the next day in the morning. It was explained to their mother that Iorela would need time to prepare the children emotionally. After all, they didn't really know her, since she hadn't seen them in over two years. Iorela told her that she also needed time to gather their clothes. Iorela explained to me that sometimes the mothers would appear when the children were about four or five, after they were toilet-trained. This way, the difficult toddler years were over, and now they could be used to work or to beg on the streets to help provide for the family. I was devastated. His six-month period of abandonment was just about to end, and if his mother visited him now, it would start over again! And what if he did well at home with her? He was a well-behaved child and didn't have the autistic tendencies that characterized many of the children at Casa Alba. I thought if she did come to get him, she would certainly keep him. Iorela told me to pray and to try not to be anxious—she didn't think I needed to worry. She would send me a message soon letting me know what had transpired.

I felt like my spirit would break. But I also knew Iorela had the welfare of the children in mind and would be wise in her handling of this matter. So I waited. And I waited. The message finally arrived—Iorela told me that when their mother returned to get Silvia and Lukas, she told her that it might be best to take the eldest child, Silvia, first. If she was able to care for Silvia, then she would want to return to take Lukas. Iorela had a feeling that their mother would have a hard time with Silvia, since she was severely autistic, and her behaviors were terribly difficult to handle. Silvia's mother picked her up in the morning, took her home, and returned several hours later. She said Silvia was too difficult to manage. She never asked Iorela if she could take Lukas. As his mother, she could take him anytime she wanted, but she didn't choose to that day. Iorela and I both were relieved as we didn't want them to live in poverty.

Time seemed to stand still. Another two months passed. Finally on April 25, 1999, I received a phone call from Romania. It was Iorela calling to tell me that Lukas was declared legally abandoned, and therefore, adoptable. This was something I had waited to hear for more than a year. She also informed me that Gusztav was also declared abandoned and adoptable. I was just as thankful for her.

The six month mark of abandonment was about to arrive for both Lukas and Guzstav. On the last day of that six month period, Iorela wondered if their mothers would stop by to visit them, and then the six-month period would begin again. Lukas' mother had only come to Casa Alba once in over three years. Iorela didn't want them to be subject to possible abuse or neglect. She decided to take both boys on a short drive into the Black Forest, also called Padurea Neagra, and she returned with them a few hours later. She anxiously waited as she wondered if their mothers would arrive. Shortly thereafter, Iorela informed me that neither mother came to the orphanage on that final day, or any day that followed.

Iorela and I decided to email each other about steps to take to adopt Gusztav, and Lukas, respectively, if single women were allowed to adopt. I wrote to her right away, but I didn't receive a response. This was not unusual, since she worked day and night, directing the orphanage and then making food, decorating special birthday cakes for each child, sewing clothes, curtains, or quilts, or repairing anything from broken toys to cars. Of course, she was from Sweden.

In May, I was excited to read her email, but wasn't prepared for the news I read that crushed my spirit with each word. A family from France was interested in adopting Lukas, and, unlike me, they had already completed their adoption papers and were ready to proceed. They were a married couple. As I still hadn't met the man of my dreams, the odds were stacked against me, as Romania still didn't allow single women to adopt.

As I drove to work that morning, a deep sadness swept over me. I imagined him being placed with a family that didn't even know him. I still prayed that God would bring him to the best family or person for him. Before I met my first patient of the day, I tried to gain my composure. The young patient asked me why I didn't look as happy as usual. I told her briefly why I was sad, and she told me that she had been adopted. She said, "Just as God brought me to the perfect family, He will guide this child to you if you are the mother he is supposed to have, or to another family who might be the best for him. But believe me, God is watching over him!"

I had to trust in that. I had to believe that Lukas would be placed in the family that was meant for him and was best for him. A few weeks later, I heard from Iorela that the family from France was no longer interested in adopting Lukas. This meant he was still available for adoption. With a great sense of relief, I continued to pray that he would someday be with me.

CHAPTER 38

OFF TO ROMANIA ONCE AGAIN

February 8, 2003—Age 7

While I was in Lukas' room and we were building with Legos, he stopped for a moment and said, "God's power is in Jesus. The devil uses his power for bad. God uses His power for good. Why are they opposites?" Then he commented, "The devil has servants that live underground just like God has angels as His servants from heaven." I had never heard of that philosophy, and never talked to him about the devil, so I wondered where he had gotten this thought.

In June of 1999, my mom, Sandi, and I began to think about going to Romania together; however, she wasn't sure she could afford to go. I encouraged her, telling her that if God wanted us to go, he would provide the money. She felt hesitant, but I told her she should write to all of her friends and family, as I would do, and ask them to support her for the trip. We were both overwhelmed by the response, and received an excess of what we would need for our travels. We knew we would bring that money along with us and give it to Lars and the foundation supporting the orphans there.

A feeling overwhelmed me that I should invite Lori Cordes—the woman I met on my trip to Kazakhstan and China—to Romania. I hadn't talked to her for more than a year, but I was able to get in touch with her. The next day, I found out she had booked a seat next to us on the plane to

Budapest. We would stay there for two weeks and mostly work with the toddlers. My mom had been a preschool teacher for more than thirty years, and I knew this would be a perfect fit since she had so much experience with young children.

On the day before I left for my trip, the last patient I had to treat was a Hispanic woman named Dolly who had an African American child with her. While talking to her, she told me that she had adopted him (something she thought would be impossible, since she was fifty, and a single woman.) She said to me, "With God, nothing is impossible!"

I shared my desires to adopt Lukas with her, and she told me that if God wanted the doors to open for him to be my son, they would open. Because I met her so close to my departure, I felt like I had just met a messenger from God to encourage me.

We met up with Lori in Atlanta. After a long flight, a four-hour train ride to Oradea from Budapest, and a car ride from Oradea to Marghita, my mom, Lori, and I settled into our bunks at Herculane late that night. I found it hard to sleep because I was so excited for both of them to experience the Swedish house that I lived in a few times and to experience the village and the people of Marghita. During our first day in Romania, my mom and I were in the kitchen at Herculane, when Lars came in. I had known him now for almost two years and quickly noticed that his calm, jovial nature was not present that day. I asked if there was something bothering him and he said, "The donations that we were expecting from Hungary were stolen at the border. That money was meant for food for the children and for paying the Romanian caregivers at the orphanage."

I asked Lars how much money was stolen and he responded, "It was about $1,200."

Interestingly, this was almost the exact amount that my mom and I had in excess from fundraising for our trip, which was amazingly a few dollars more than $1,200.

I said to Lars, "Well, my mom and I have a gift that we brought from the States." I went into the bunk room and got the money and handed it to him, telling him the amount. Lars was a stoic man, and I had never seen him with a sense of vulnerability, but as he received this money, tears welled up in his eyes. God's amazing grace and provision was displayed when it was most needed.

November 2002—Age 6

Lukas and I were in the car and had just driven past several stores. He asked me, "What's the closest store in the world?" I answered, "Albertson's," which is our local grocery store. I asked him what he thought and he said, "Jesus." I asked him what he meant, and he said, "He gives us all the food we need and all the clothes we need. Jesus gives us everything we need so he's the closest store in the world."

CHAPTER 39

THE ULTIMATE DECISION

Shortly after I arrived in Romania, Iorela and I had just finished eating a meal at Herculane and she let me know she had some exciting news for me. She said, "Single women in Romania are allowed to adopt children here. Single men still are not, but women are. We will need to talk soon about whether or not you are serious about adopting Lukas." I had been told by a Romanian volunteer that single women were discouraged from adopting so I hadn't thought it would be possible for me.

For the next two days, I knew I was about to make the biggest decision of my life. I wanted the best for Lukas. As I walked up the steps at Casa Alba, I wondered again if Lukas would recognize me. After all, it had been eight months since I had seen him. I saw him in the dining room and immediately walked over and picked him up and held him in my arms. One of the workers asked, "Cine este?"— "Who is this?" Lukas' eyes lit up with excitement as he said, "Kitty." I was so surprised that he remembered me, and I smiled so wide my cheeks hurt.

Later that evening back at Herculane, I was able to talk about the possibility of adopting Lukas with Iorela and one of the Swedish volunteers named Daniel Persson. Although I had not met him on previous trips to Marghita, I had heard wonderful things about him from Iorela. The three of us sat at the large kitchen table late into the night as he provided me with information about Lukas that he had learned while working at Casa Alba. He encouraged me to follow my instincts, and if that lead me toward Lukas, so be it. He had been to Marghita several times to work with the children and probably knew some of them better than I, and I respected his input.

During that trip, Iorela needed me to care mostly for the "babies" as many of the Swedish volunteers had returned to Sweden for a vacation. This meant I didn't get to care for Lukas as often during this essential time while I was trying to make my big decision. One evening, when I had to go into a separate room and care for the babies, Lukas found me and said, "No babies—stay here," in Romanian. He was strongly letting me know that I was to have "zero" contact with the babies, and that he wanted all of my attention. Much to his chagrin, this wasn't possible since I wasn't assigned to work with the children in his room.

We weren't able to bond as often as we had in the past, which allowed me to make a more rational decision, and not just an emotional one. I watched him with two amazing caregivers, Tina and Lidia, and I thought to myself, "I can't take him from his people." I kept thinking this—that I would be taking him from a culture, a language, and a people he knew and loved. I prayed and prayed, and went on a long walk by myself, asking for direction to do the best thing for him. I continued to think, "I can't take him from his people."

One day, Iorela asked my mom and me to join her as she was going to bring a new baby from the hospital to Casa Alba. My mom and I entered the room to find Georgy lying in his crib, silent. While reaching in to pick him up, my mom couldn't help but notice that the mattress was saturated in urine. His cheeks were mottled with a rash as a result of lying on this wet, moldy mattress. As Iorela got everything ready to clean him up, my mom handed him to me for a minute and she lifted up the mattress so she could clean it for the next child. She found that its bottom was covered in a black mold. Once again, we were so thankful that we could bring Georgy to Casa Alba and provide the nurturing environment that he needed.

August 30, 2003—Age 7

One night, I was telling Lukas that I was going to pray for my friend who miscarried her baby. Lukas knew that she was pregnant, and I wanted to explain about her loss. He replied, "It's OK, Mom, God can take care of the baby better than we can. He knows what the baby needs when it cries because He understands baby language."

CHAPTER 40

SWEET SUMMERTIME

Romania in the summer was vastly different than in winter. There was vibrant color in the trees and in the fields that had once stood dismal and barren. The warm, balmy air invited everyone to take a trip outdoors, while the frigid, winter air seemed to suggest that guests weren't welcome. Daniel and I would take the toddlers out to play in sandboxes and would enjoy picnics with the entire staff—including all twenty-four of the children at Casa Alba—up in the hillside just outside of town. And there was fruit, and plenty of it. Not just an apple, as was the only available fruit in the winter. The kids and I ate watermelon one hot day and they would cheer, "lebenita" "lebenita"—their toddler-style name for the balloon-shaped fruit—while the pink juice trickled down their cheeks. New life was brought to these precious children just by the new foods that were available to them at this time of year.

Iorela also took us on a one hour trip to a large building in the Black Forest, which was part of Transylvania. It served as a summertime retreat for vacationers many years prior. During our drive, we passed hundreds of acres of wheat and sunflower fields. We passed rolling hills with gorgeous fields for farming and small mountains with lush trees enveloping the road we traversed. I could see why the natives would be so proud of their beautiful country. It saddened me to think that one horrible dictator could strip families away from their beautiful farms and claim the land and its children for his own in an attempt to gain control and build his army.

Life in the summer was in such wonderful contrast to the bleak, dreary days of winter. The weather was warm and balmy, and if the temperatures reached certain peaks, my mom and I would come home to Herculane to find Lars and Lukas and Gusztav and Otto, bathing in their swimsuits in a giant wine barrel. The pure joy on the faces of Lars and the children was enough to warm my heart for the rest of the year. A simple change in seasons brought so much healing to these children, many who had rickets and other ailments due to lack of sunlight. I was never so thankful, as I was at that moment, for a season such as summer.

CHAPTER 41

THE CHILD WITH EMPTY EYES

September 28, 2006—Age 10

Lukas was talking to me as we were getting ready in the morning and he said, "Do you know who the lucky ones are? The lucky ones are the young kids who die early." Surprised by his statement, I asked him what he meant. He said, "They are close to God, then they are here on earth a short time, then they're with God again when they die. It's hard to be on earth as an adult with all this fighting—it's not going to stop." This was quite a weighty discussion for a ten-year-old, or anyone for that matter—talking about the young dying and global war. I never thought of the children who died young as the "lucky ones." He, as a child, was resolute about this thought. Also, the idea he had, that the children are with God before they are born, was something I hadn't thought about before. I was left speechless.

Lori and my mom were naturals with the children. On our first day, one of the babies named April immediately drew our attention. She had been burned with a cigarette all over her torso, head and mouth. When we inquired about these burns, we were horrified by what we learned. When mothers brought their healthy babies to the hospital to abandon them, which was not unusual in this region, the hospital staff told them they did not have room for healthy children. Unless the child was sick or hurt, the hospital couldn't care for them. April's mother was desperate, and burned her with a cigarette, then broke her arm so that the hospital would accept her. This was almost too much to bear. Casa Alba quickly told the hospital that they could care for her, and we arrived shortly after she was placed to live at Casa Alba.

April's face was expressionless, as if she was devoid of spirit. She did not laugh or smile, and made no eye contact. When she did, it was if she stared straight through one's soul. Lori felt especially drawn to April during our trip there, and she dedicated every hour of her time at Casa Alba to her. Lori would arrive at the orphanage, and hold April, sing to her and pray for her. She would stroke her little arms and legs and smile and laugh while she tried to engage her in play. April was sixteen months old, yet couldn't hold her head up, roll over or sit. She had little muscle tone. For the first week, April showed no expression, no life, no response that let us know that she had any spirit within her. Lori persisted in love and care. Every chance she had, she poured her heart into loving that child.

Then it happened. One day, while Lori was tickling April, she laughed. April laughed so heartily that we were astonished. My mom and I were in the room, and we were accustomed to hearing only Lori's voice. April was usually completely, and sadly silent, but we sat in amazement at the sound that came from her. April continued to laugh and smile, the most beautiful smile that we had ever seen. Her once lifeless eyes now sparkled with joy!

The three of us knew that day why Lori had come to Romania. It was for April. The love that Lori showered on her awakened her spirit! We thanked God for this miracle—it may have been small, but for this precious child, it gave her life.

CHAPTER 42

BUNK-BED REVELATION

February 7, 2007—Age 11

Lukas and I were sitting on the couch and he said, "I have another thought. The sun is like a black hole close to the earth and whenever God touches it, it becomes light. His hand guides it around as it gives light." He caused me to look at everything on earth in a new "light."

Two days after Iorela asked me to decide about Lukas' adoption, the thought swept over me again, "I can't take him from his people." I was praying for an answer as I sat in my bunk at Herculane, the Swedish volunteer house. I opened my Bible randomly and came upon a verse from Exodus 6 that said, "I will take you for My people, and I will be your God, I am the Lord who brought you out from the burdens." Just then, I felt my answer was clear. A peaceful confidence settled into my heart that I could adopt Lukas, as I had desired and dreamed of for almost two years.

The next day at a marketplace in Oradea, a city an hour's drive from Marghita, I sat with Iorela and Gusztav, Lukas' roommate, whom Iorela was trying to adopt. I told her that I was sure I wanted to adopt Lukas. The peace I had while reading that fateful scripture remained with me as I told her my decision.

The day before I was to return to America, Iorela contacted an adoption worker in Bucharest named Dr. Dan Mihaiesi to ask him questions about Lukas' adoption. He said that there was nothing I could do to facilitate his adoption. I had to wait to see if he was placed on a list for international adoption with the U.S. If he wasn't, there was nothing I could do to get him out of the country. My heart sank with this news.

Before I left Romania, I went to Casa Alba to say goodbye to the children and to Lukas. I noticed that a pair of maroon and white-striped leggings belonging to Lukas were beginning to get ragged. They were hand-me-downs from Karcsi, who wore them during "gymnastika," and from some other child to Karsci before that. They were simply worn out. These pants reminded me of both boys, both whom I loved so much. Later, I asked Iorela if I could have just a swatch of those leggings. She understood. She cut a piece of the scarlet cloth from the bottom of the pants so that I could remember the sweet times we shared. I placed it in my devotional as a bookmark to remind me to pray through Lukas' adoption process. It has remained there until this day and is a reminder of God's precious blessing to me.

CHAPTER 43

LETTERS TO LUKAS

I wrote this entry into Lukas' personal book on August 11, the day before we left to return home:

Dear Lukas,

This is the third time I've been to Casa Alba, and each time I grow fonder of you.

My name is Kristi Wilkinson and I'm from America. You may not realize it, but I've been praying for you for almost two years now. I wanted to tell you that you have a loving spirit and that from age two to three-and-a-half, you loved to be held. I knew this back in December when I first met you in 1997. I had a working shift through the night several times, and each time, I'd pray that if you needed to be held, you'd wake up while I was there. Interestingly, each night shift, you would wake up and I would go to your room and rock you to sleep as I held you. You'd lift your head every once in awhile just to make sure I was still there. I wanted you to know that wherever life takes you, I wish you the most joy, and I will always remember you. I love you and pray that God blesses you. Your picture rests on my nightstand next to my bed in Denver, CO, and your smile will always bring joy to me.

God bless, Kristi

My mom wrote the next entry in Lukas' book, dated the same day:

Dear Lukas,

I'm Kristi's mom and this was my first visit to Casa Alba. I had heard about you and had seen your picture, so you were the first one I recognized. You cuddled up in my arms the first time I held you, and I knew what Kristi meant when she told me how precious you were. Every time someone held you, you always looked so contented. When you find a new home, you will make some new family very happy, and you will at last be in the arms of those who will love you forever! God bless you little one, Kristi's mama, Sandi

CHAPTER 44

ADOPTION HURDLES

August 31, 2003—Age 7

Lukas and I were in the car near our home and he said, "The cross makes all of this work." I asked, "What work?" He answered, "All of this—the clouds, the air, the trees—it's what makes all of this work. The best part of the cross is the front side because Jesus was lying on the front side. That's the side that overcomes bad and evil, not the back side." Then he thought for a while and said, "I prayed to God that I could be wise and smart, to teach people like Elijah, Paul, and John, to teach how God loves us."

When we got home, he said, "God told me in my dream, God's going to give me a present of good. He told me what my job should be. He wants me to be a fireman or to save people. I'll be too scared. Do you think he'd let me scoop ice cream instead?" This conversation was pretty heavy for me. I once again asked where he got these thoughts, and he said—as he had before—"God speaks it to my brain." I had never thought about the front vs. the back-side of the cross. Because he sat in church with me to listen to the first few songs and then went to Sunday school class with me to teach the two-year-olds, I knew that I had never talked about the front vs. the back-side of the cross and their respective meanings. His comments got me to think about Jesus' sacrifice on a new level. His concepts about the cross bringing meaning to the sky and the clouds and everything on earth challenged me and my faith to seek God even more.

I returned to the states in early August and after a few days, I began to call adoption agencies in Denver to see if I could truly adopt Lukas, as Romania still had strict conditions for international adoption. I called every agency listed in the phonebook, from Denver to Colorado Springs to Estes Park, but none could help me. One helped with U.S. adoptions only, and one aided in international, but not Romanian adoptions. Others helped with Romanian adoptions, but not through Casa Alba, Lukas' orphanage. I remember my frustration reaching an all-time high, and I thought I would be forced to give up my dream.

That week, I received a call from a woman from Denver—Karleen Dewey—who worked with the foundation and the children in Marghita. She said, "I hear you are interested in adopting Lukas." I told her about my difficulty finding an agency, and she replied, "Instead of asking yourself if you should do this, you should be asking yourself why not?" She continued to encourage me to press forward, as she was an adoptive mother and knew the trials that came with the process.

That night, a thought came to me: I would try one more thing, and if that didn't work, his adoption would not be possible. That "one more thing" was to call a woman named Liz who lived in Maryland. She had adopted one of Lukas' former roommates, Imre, and another little girl from Casa Alba named Anna Maria. I would ask her what she did to make their adoptions possible. I sent an email to Iorela in Romania and kept my fingers crossed that she would have Liz's information. Iorela responded quickly with her email address, and through this, I was able to get her phone number. I prayed that she would be home, since I knew her family had just moved from Germany to Maryland for a new military assignment.

To my good fortune, she answered the phone and remembered meeting me. We had only met for one day in Romania on my second trip in October of 1998. She had traveled from Germany to Romania after hearing of the plight of the children. She was so excited that I had called, saying that my previous email, asking for her phone number, brought her to tears due to a recent memory at Casa Alba. When she went to adopt

Imre and Anna Maria, Lukas ran up to her calling her, "Kitty, Kitty," since her back was to him, and her blonde ponytail and her build resembled mine. When she turned around to face Lukas, she noticed that he became so sad when he realized that she was not his "Kitty." Because she was a witness to the bond that we shared, she encouraged me to try everything possible to adopt him.

Liz proceeded to give me the number of the adoption agency she used in Connecticut, and told me to call a woman there named Elizabeth Kendrick, who had helped her. She ended the phone conversation by saying, "You were lucky to reach me today, as I will going to the hospital tomorrow to have surgery. My balance has been terrible and the tests showed that I will need surgery for my cerebellum." I was so thankful for God's timing in allowing me to speak to her the day before surgery—brain surgery no less. I was in awe!

That same day, I called Elizabeth Kendrick, and she returned my call the following day while I was at work. She asked a question that would send me over the first hurdle, which was my age. I had to be at least twenty-five years older than Lukas. Luckily I was thirty-two by then, he was still three—one hurdle down, two to go. Next, she asked if Lukas was an infant. Thankfully for me he was not. If he was a baby, I would not be able to adopt, as infants were reserved solely for married couples. I told her that he was almost four, and she replied it was a "positive" thing that he was older than two. I jumped hurdle two. Lastly, and possibly the biggest hurdle of all, she asked if Lukas was on the "list." All I knew was that Lukas was not yet on "it." This list was one for American adoptions. She commented that when we began our conversation, she was pessimistic about my chances, but after speaking with me, she was hopeful. She told me to find an agency in Denver that would be able to process some of the paperwork.

The very next day at work, my first patient of the day told me that she was a social worker. I asked her where she worked. She said she had done work for adoptions in the past, although she was currently retired. I asked her where she had done the adoption work and she gave me the name of an agency called Adoption Alliance, which was only a few miles from my work in Aurora, Colorado. Once again, it seemed like things were falling into my lap. I didn't even have to search through the yellow pages this time for a Denver-based agency.

CHAPTER 45

ANSWERS ON THE ROOFTOP

October 2002—Age 6

Lukas and I were on a walk in our neighborhood near a hillside where a new house was being built. We noticed piles of rocks strewn across the street. The rocks obviously came from sandbags that lined the property to prevent runoff in the streets from the recent rain. It was also obvious that mischievous kids had dumped the rocks into the street to damage people's car tires. We had the idea to clean up the rocks before any more damage could be done. As we were picking up the rocks and carrying them back onto the property, Lukas noticed the frame of the house with construction vehicles in place. He started talking about ideas and inventions that people have, and he stopped and stated, "I know our brain is ours, but when we get a new idea to make something or build something, it really comes from God. We finally say, 'I got it'. But the idea comes from God." I asked him where he had gotten that idea, as I always thought I came up with creative ideas on my own. He confidently replied again, "God is speaking it to my brain."

A little while later, after we were finished cleaning up all of the rocks, he asked me why people do horrible things like we had just witnessed. Then he said, "I know it was boys who threw those rocks. That was evil, Mom. Evil is like an insect getting into the body and it starts to control the body. I pray that I will

not do evil things like that." I walked away from that property
with two new insights, one on creative ideas and their inception,
and the other, on the insidious nature of evil.

The night I had called Adoption Alliance, I prayed and wondered if I would be the best mom for Lukas, and if I could give him what he needed since I would be a single mom. After I asked God to speak to me, I opened my bible randomly. My eyes were drawn to the words from Isaiah 54, "O, ye barren woman without child, I will bless you it is as if you had more than one child," and I slept peacefully that night.

Shortly after that—since family members and friends questioned if adoption was a good idea for me—I went out onto a flat-roofed surface, accessible from my bedroom window, for some solitary time. I only wanted to talk to God, but I brought my cordless phone—there were no cell phones at the time. I had the phone because I was expecting a phone call from my doctor's office about a worrisome bug bite I had gotten while in Romania. Although I had been home about a week, the bite was not only getting larger and more red, it had a ring around it reminiscent of Lyme's disease, and I wanted the doctor to quell my worries. I asked God to continue to speak to me, as I wanted to do what He wanted for Lukas. I started to read my bible again, beginning with Psalm 1. As I came to Psalm 10, my eyes were drawn to the words, "For I am the helper of the orphan." Seconds later the phone rang. It was Elizabeth from the adoption agency. It didn't matter that the doctor hadn't called. My worries washed away. Before she said another word, peace filled my spirit and I felt I knew God wanted Lukas to be my son!

Elizabeth told me she had spoken to the adoption worker from Romania named Dr. Dan Mihaiesi, the same man who told Iorela that I could do nothing to influence Lukas' adoption process. He told Elizabeth that we would soon know if the judge placed Lukas on the "list" for U.S. adoption. When I asked her if I should start any paperwork, she said no, that I needed to wait. If Lukas wasn't on the U.S. "list," there was nothing I could do to adopt him. This was devastating to me—the process seemed truly impossible.

In the middle of August, Iorela called me again and said to me, "Are you sure you want to adopt Lukas, because the adoption worker says it will be difficult. If you want Lukas, we are going to have to fight for this." I confirmed with her the answer I knew in my heart, "Yes."

Iorela decided to take matters into her own hands and called Dr. Dan Mihaiesi. He worked for the adoption agency called Copii Lumii, which meant "Children of the World," and Iorela had a working relationship with him because he had facilitated the adoption process for several other children from Casa Alba. She also knew that if Lukas didn't get onto the national list for adoption with his agency, it would be close to impossible for me to adopt Lukas. Of the many adoption agencies in Romania, it was the only one known to Iorela that was linked to a U.S. adoption agency. I already mentioned the difficulty I experienced when I called every adoption agency listed in Colorado, and found none that handled Romanian adoptions!

She emphatically said to Dr. Dan, "You need to get Lukas on your national list! Kristi knows and loves him, and wants to adopt him."

Dr. Dan replied, "This is not how it works Iorela. I have no say or control in this matter. He has been put on a national list, but there are many adoption agencies, and Lukas could be assigned to any of these agencies. It is a random placement—I cannot choose which child gets placed on which list!"

Iorela replied firmly, "This needs to be done. Who can I speak with to make sure that Lukas gets on your list?" Iorela was like a female lioness defending her cubs—he didn't stand a chance. With frustration in his voice and a huff exasperation, he gave her the number of a female social worker in Bucharest.

Without hesitation, Iorela called this woman. She was also familiar with Iorela, who always fought for the best interest of the children. The agency originally did not require that the families come to Casa Alba to pick up their children. Marghita was far away from any city and to access it, one needed to travel by planes, trains, and automobiles— a costly inconvenience for the agencies. This did not matter to Iorela. She believed that it was important for the future parents to see the orphanage where the children had been raised, to meet the caregivers, to receive the picture books, and also to experience the farewell party that was given to each of the adopted children. Iorela also believed it was important for the children at Casa Alba to see their roommates with their new loving and caring parents. Dr. Dan at first resisted this, but due to Iorela's persistence, he came to Casa Alba. After his trip to Casa Alba, he agreed that Iorela's protocol was necessary for the children and the families. From this, the female social worker in Bucharest became familiar with Iorela and her commitment to the children.

With assertion in her voice, Iorela said to her, "Lukas needs to be on your list! How can you get this done?"

The woman replied with an answer that mimicked Dr. Dan's answer. She stated, "This is not how it is done. The children can be placed with any of the many adoption agencies that we have here. Iorela, there is nothing I can do."

Iorela did not accept this answer. She replied firmly, "No, Lukas needs to be placed on your list! Krist has worked here with him since he was two. She has a strong bond with him and he with her. Kristi wants to adopt him and we need to see to it that he is placed on your list." The social worker still insisted that there was not much that she could do.

Iorela later told me that she phoned this woman several times to emphasize the need for Lukas to be placed on her agencies' list. Then, she told me to wait and pray, and that I should hear from her soon.

About two weeks later, on August 23, 1999, Iorela received a call from Dr. Dan. With surprise and excitement in his voice he said, "Iorela, Lukas is on my list!"

Iorela immediately called me from a phone booth in Oradea, with Gusztav crouched beside her, to tell me the news I was eager to hear—Lukas was on Dr. Dan's list for his Romanian agency, Copii Lumii. Now, we needed to wait to see if Lukas would be placed on the list for international U.S. adoption. Unfortunately, this decision was not in Dan's hands.

I waited and waited again. Finally, on September 9th, Iorela called me at 6:30 in the morning and said the words I had waited years to hear, "Kristi, you are going to be a mother. Lukas was placed on the list for U.S. adoption and is linked with your adoption agency." Since the judge in Romania, who chose Lukas' future homeland, had no idea a girl in Denver was praying for him to be on that list, I thanked God for this miraculous orchestration that would change my life. Then, Gusztav got on the phone to tell me Lukas was waiting for me, and after I hung up the phone with Iorela, I began to cry tears of gratitude.

After work that day on September 9, I was asked to attend a mission team meeting at my church in Denver to tell them about my latest trip to Romania. One of the women on the team—also one of my patients at the time—asked me to mention that Lukas had just been placed on the list for U.S. adoption. I hesitated, as I didn't feel the adoption was the focus of the meeting, but my patient insisted I mention it. The minister, Keith Andrews, took time at the end of the meeting to pray for Lukas and me. He prayed that all the paperwork would go smoothly, and if it were God's will, that the doors would continue to open, allowing Lukas to be my son.

I drove home from the meeting, filled with joy and anticipation. But since I hadn't even told my family, I was eager to get home to call them. As I walked up the steps to my apartment, I noticed my neighbor Rita Bastien—who lived in the bottom unit of the house—sitting on the front porch. Not in the mood for small talk, I wanted to bound up the steps to my apartment, but I paused for a minute. She asked, "Is everything OK? I heard you crying this morning and I just had to ask."

Surprised that she could hear me through the apartment walls, since I lived above her, I affirmed that everything was OK. I told her that I was crying because a small boy I had cared for from Romania had made the list for U.S. adoption. When she overheard me crying in the morning, I had just received the news. I explained that I had been praying about this adoption for almost two years, and I would finally get to start the process. She asked me what I needed to do next, and I mentioned that I was told I had to get an application from Immigration and Naturalization Service (INS), and that I didn't know where to find this office.

She then replied, "Did you know that I have worked for INS with adoptions for the past fifteen years, and I can get the application for you tomorrow?" Also, she added, "I worked with a woman who is the Secretary to the U.S. Ambassador in Romania, so if you need help along the way, I can contact her!"

I could hardly believe her words, spoken just shortly after the minister's prayer at church. I didn't know whether to laugh or cry. I was amazed at how everything was coming together, like pieces of a puzzle. But I couldn't cry yet. I had to call my parents with the news. I got in touch with my dad and told him that Lukas made the list for American adoption. Then, I shared the details about Rita working on adoptions at the INS, and he said, "Kristi, if I were doubting you, or had been skeptical before, I can stop asking questions now. I support your decision."

CHAPTER 46

THE ARDUOUS ROAD TO ADOPTION

September 12, 2002—Age 6

Lukas and I were taking a late evening walk just before he went to bed and he looked at the moon and commented, "The moon is a lamp in God's house and the rooms are in the clouds." I reflected on this image from Lukas' perspective and tried to picture it for myself. I hoped I would get to see that lamp and all of the rooms as he saw it someday.

I had taken a premature trip to the adoption agency, Adoption Alliance in Denver, to pick up preliminary paperwork just in case I would need it. The minute I arrived at work the next day, I faxed in the one-page document to begin my process. This included a few more tests regarding my financial ability to support a child. Linda Donovan, from Adoption Alliance, called me before the end of the day to tell me that they approved this first step immediately, and asked when I could come in for an interview. She commented that if I couldn't meet with her the following Tuesday, September 14, "I won't have another day available until mid-October." Without hesitation, I booked that day in September—it just so happened that I had Tuesdays off from work.

I drove to the agency from work to pick up the second application from Linda.

It was one inch thick! She said, "Don't get overwhelmed by the size of the application. It will take you a few months to finish." I had an overwhelming feeling that I didn't have a few months to complete the application. There was a sense of urgency that told me I needed to finish it as quickly as possible.

I opened the application and noted that it included a physical exam, an autobiography, several essays, personal recommendations, and a police background check, to name a few items. The first stumbling block surfaced when I called my doctor's office. The secretary informed me that the next available visit was a few months from then. The next day at work, I bumped into Dr. Spees, a co-worker at Spalding Rehab, and told him my plight. He said, "Call my office and tell the staff I can see you any time tomorrow." Of course, that was on a Tuesday—my day off!

That weekend's endeavor would be to complete my ten-page autobiography. Since I didn't have a computer or printer of my own, I spent ten straight hours at my friend, Inger Lamb's house, sitting at her computer, delving into every nook and cranny of my past. It included thirty-some intricate psychological questions, several that asked about the most difficult parts of my childhood. Honestly and gratefully, I really didn't have any "difficult parts," as I grew up in wonderful household with supportive parents.

Julie was my only sister, and we had always been very close. The only abnormal thing about our childhood was that we didn't fight like typical siblings. We had separate bedrooms, but on many nights, we chose to share a room until we were out of elementary school. We grew up doing gymnastics together, and could be found in the hallway or bedroom doing cartwheels or supporting each other as we learned to do handstands. The only negative memory I could dredge up for the autobiography was when Julie was experimenting with the fan in our bedroom one humid summer day. She stuck my stuffed monkey's hand inside the fan, swiftly amputating his finger. I was sure they wouldn't count this against us when reviewing my application!

The autobiography was also supposed to include the stability of my parents. My Dad, Jim, was a teacher and coach for twenty-three years at the high school that I also attended. He coached the varsity basketball team at Abington High—which was in the suburbs of Philadelphia—and he invited the players to our house on Saturdays throughout the year. Many of them came from poor African-American families, and he welcomed them into our home as if they were his own sons. He hosted them for "lasagna night" and then would entertain them with music or games in the living room. I would find him sitting at our old-fashioned player piano, tricking them into thinking he played like a professional. I remember walking into the living room, finding high school teenagers with my Dad's headphones on, listening to or singing songs from Frank Sinatra or the Carpenter's, his favorite musicians at the time.

To say that he was a popular teacher would be an understatement. Kids petitioned to be in his class, as he was a master storyteller. Some female seniors were known to cry if they didn't get him as a teacher. He played sports with me and my sister throughout our childhood, and kids in the neighborhood would even knock on the door and say, "Is your Dad ready to come out and play?" He was the pitcher of summer softball that we played almost every night with other neighborhood kids. He was also "it" in the game of "chase" on many nights, and joined in during kick-the-can- as well. My dad truly was a wonderful role model, so I didn't have anything deprecating to say about him as a father.

My mom was known by one of our friends as "Saint Sandi," and I think I know why. She was always helping others. Once, when one young teacher couldn't afford his rent, my mom had the idea that he could live in a room in our attic until he was financially stable. Later, after hearing about an African-American family whose house burned down, they lived with us until they had a new home. Also, when my sister and I were teenagers, my mom found out about a man who had just gotten out of a Polish refugee camp. He needed a place to stay. For the next several years, he lived with us, even becoming a fixture at my dad's basketball games. Although his surname ended in "ski," we referred to him as Jerry "Wilkinson," a member of the family. Perhaps this was not a "normal" way to live, with others of different ethnicities living in the bedroom next to mine, but this is how I was raised.

Next, I had to find two non-family members of an older generation whom I had known for more than twenty years to write recommendation letters. I called my childhood friend, Jean Oxendine, and she said that her dad, Dr. Joe Oxendine, wouldn't hesitate, since he had known me since

I was two years old. He wrote the letter that week. My friend, Sharon Okamoto—whom I had known since seventh grade—affirmed that her mom, Susanne, would be more than happy to write a recommendation letter. Susanne was like a second mother to me and had been following my journey's overseas throughout the years. She happily replied that she would support me with this process.

I was on a mission and finished the application in five days. When I walked into the agency to hand them my paperwork—including the ten-page autobiography—work and insurance verification, the receptionist questioned, "Are you having problems with the application?"

I replied, "No, I am finished with the application."

The receptionist replied, "You can't be finished with the entire application. No one had ever finished it in under three months!

I repeated that I completed everything that was needed. I had an urgency; I didn't know what was pushing me, but something told me I needed to do this as fast as I could. Although surprised, they accepted my application and told me a home study was next.

The home visit was booked within two weeks and would include several visits, for up to ten hours, to ascertain my ability to be a parent and provide a good home for a child. The woman assigned to do my home study was named Donna. She arrived at my apartment, and she asked me to share my story of how I came to meet Lukas. After one hour, she had tears in her eyes and said, "I want you to be able to adopt this child. I will not be the stumbling block in this adoption."

As the paperwork was being processed, the agency asked for money every time I turned around to cover the costs of checking my background, processing my paperwork, and contacting and filling out forms for international adoption. My checking account was down to the tune of forty dollars, and I knew that if I passed my home study, a large sum of money would be required. About that time, my friend Bill called to discuss the house I had bought just over a year ago, and that he had agreed to renovate. (After the completion of his renovations, we had tenants living in the house.) Bill proceeded to say, "We have to sell the house. I am going to move to Texas and we need to sell the house now!" The timing was perfect for me, because I needed to come up with $15,000 within the next few months, if not weeks. I already knew from my friend who worked at the bank that I could not get a loan for that amount. So, we put the "For Sale" sign in the front yard, and I prayed that in the year-and-a-half that we'd owned it, the market would be in our favor.

At the same time, two neighboring houses were also for sale; this was not an opportune time to be trying to sell our house. To say that I was on edge would be an understatement. Within a week, our house had piqued the interest of a few people. In no time, a young woman submitted an offer. Interestingly, I found out that she also had attended University of Richmond. After splitting the profit with Bill, I would profit slightly more that $15,000—the exact amount I desperately needed to adopt Lukas! For me, this was a miracle!

By November 17, I received approval from the Denver-based agency to adopt Lukas. Immigration's approval was next. There was an unexpected delay, and my fingerprints were lost. I was not worried, as I had never been featured on *America's Most Wanted*. I bumped into my downstairs neighbor Rita, who worked at INS, and she said that she would be able to call the FBI headquarters in West Virginia and try to locate them. I certainly would not have been able to intervene with the FBI otherwise. Rita was successful in locating the fingerprints; they were processed in record time, or so a woman at the FBI reported to Rita.

The next step was to fill out more documents to extend Lukas' association with my agency. The only problem was, I needed my passport number to complete the extension. But the INS had my passport and I didn't have the number written anywhere. I called Rita once again, and she was able to track down my passport number at INS. Once again, a small, but crucial step in this process was solved with ease.

Rita found out that Romania was going to increase the cost of international adoptions by $5,000, at the start of the year 2000. She said to me, "I just wanted to let you know that I flagged your chart at INS to process your paperwork before the end of December so you won't have to pay the extra $5,000. It's out of my hands now, but I hope it works."

I was so thankful. Rita had done this extra work for me so willingly, without being asked. I spent that last $700 that I had in the bank buying the house. I would have the money to adopt Lukas, but I didn't have an extra $5,000 sitting around.

I received a letter in the mail on January 28 from Romania with the U.S. Embassy written on the envelope. I was so nervous to open it. Since it was so late in January, I assumed that I didn't get my papers processed in time for the end-of-the-year deadline, and that they were asking me to send the extra $5,000. What I read next was amazing.

I carefully opened the letter and read the most beautiful words I could ever have imagined—the U.S. Embassy had approved me to be the adoptive mother of Lukas, "effective December 31, 1999." Rita had done it once again! I was approved on the last possible day of the year, and would avoid the extra $5,000 that I couldn't afford. Now I just had to wait for the Romanian court to decide. I wasn't anxious as I could sense God's hand at work!

Within a day, I was asked to fill out another "extension" for Lukas' adoption papers. Why the powers that be didn't realize that this process included a bunch of red-tape, I will never know. But I had to comply. I had only six days to return my extension, and this meant it needed to be received by February 4. This time, they required that I have Lukas' medical record number to complete the extension form. I contacted the adoption agency in Connecticut to get this number, and the next day at 8:00 a.m., the secretary informed me that the FAX containing his medical number had come through. I needed to have it notarized. Since I was at work, I wasn't sure what to do. But I asked a woman if there were any notaries, and she knew a notary who worked in human resources. I had it notarized at work, but of course could not simply FAX it back. It had to be sent immediately by Fed-Ex back to Connecticut with the original notary seal on it. Time was running out.

Luckily for me, my 8:00 a.m. patient cancelled due to a snow storm, affording me a short amount of time to run out and try to find a post office. I drove to the post office in the storm, hardly able to see ten feet in front of me, but unfortunately, it didn't open until 9:00 am. I didn't have an hour to wait. A woman in the parking lot noticed that I was running around frantically out in the snow, and she asked if she could help me.

I told her that I needed to send something by Fed-Ex, and I didn't know where to do this. She said, "Oh, I can open my craft store early for you, and I can send it for you. I just opened a shipping center in my store." I felt a pit in my stomach as I opened my wallet to find sixteen dollars, and no credit cards. She said, "It will cost $15.75." A feeling of thankfulness settled over me. Not only had this woman recognized that I needed help, but I had also found the time and money to do just what I needed, during the middle of my work-day. Now I just needed to pray for the Romanian judge to approve Lukas' adoption.

On February 15, 2000, I called the adoption agency in Connecticut to talk to a woman named Nancy Aker who was processing my case. I was calling to ask her some questions about yet another form I needed to fill out. She replied, "It is interesting that you called this morning because the Romanian court just approved for you to adopt Lukas yesterday, February 14."

I could hardly believe her words: A dream that I had since Christmas time of 1997 was finally to become reality. It didn't matter that I wouldn't be receiving chocolates from the boyfriend I didn't have—this was the best Valentine's Day gift ever! That night I opened my devotional to read before I went to sleep. The swatch from Lukas' hand-me-down maroon and white-striped pants that I used as a bookmark fell from the book. As I held on to it, I felt that God truly was blessing me with the desires of my heart.

I continued to pray for Lukas that this process wouldn't be upsetting for him. The adoption agency informed me that there was another step. What was it now? I would have to wait another two to three weeks for the local Romanian court to approve Lukas' adoption. The main court in Bucharest wasn't enough. Then I would be given the dates that I could travel to Romania with my mother to bring Lukas home to America.

The news finally came that Lukas would become my son on March 21, the court date in Romania when the adoption would be final. I could hardly believe that everything was processed in about seven months, since some adoptions can take years. Shortly after this, I received an email from Iorela that her court date to adopt Gusztav was set. We found out during our next phone conversation that our court dates were the same. Both boys would receive mothers on the same day!

There was yet another waiting period. I wouldn't find out my dates of travel for a few more weeks, which would most likely have me in Romania sometime in April. Interestingly, Iorela told me that Lukas asked her earlier, "Will I go to America in April?" as if he somehow knew. I felt so blessed and honored that he would be my son. I almost needed to pinch myself to see if I were dreaming.

Lukas was legally approved as my son in the court in Oradea on March 21 at 11:00 a.m. Just ten minutes later, in the same courthouse, Gusztav was approved as Iorela's son—I couldn't have imagined that happening in my wildest dreams. After a waiting period that ended April 17, we would find out our immigration dates in Bucharest. Then, for Lukas and me it would be home to America, and to Sweden for Iorela and Gusztav. Spalding Rehab granted me a family leave of absence, and I would return to work after three-months of one-on one- time with Lukas. The head of human resources told me that as she knew adoptions could be complicated and lengthy, she wouldn't start my three-month leave until my feet hit the ground in America.

There were many skeptics who did not think this adoption was a very good idea. Many people close to me had my best interest in mind, thinking that it would be difficult to afford and make it more difficult to find a husband someday. My sister, Julie, however had doubts for other reasons. She was worried about my ability to handle a young boy while I had full-time work. She also was concerned that I wouldn't have enough help to raise him as a single mom in Denver, so far from my family in San Diego. But, as my older sister, I knew she was trying to protect me. A few friends— including Heather Neely, from PT school at Hahnemann—walked through the process with me with no doubts. Heather just so happened to share the same birthday as Lukas. She had a confidence, saying months before the adoption was finalized, "I think this little buddy is going to be yours." My college roommate, Scottie Hill Belfi, also encouraged me by praying for him since the day I first told her about him. She wrote a recommendation letter for me that helped me to become his mother and she would later become a Godmother to him. Another friend, Jean Williams, gave me a journal before my first trip to Romania. She had the insight to tell me that I should write about my journey and every detail of his adoption in case it did come to fruition. It was because of that journal that I had chronicled so many amazing events that I could share with Lukas and others.

CHAPTER 47

SHOWERED WITH LOVE

December 27, 2003—Age 8

Lukas guessed this date—December 27—as the birth date, along with the sex of my sister Julie's first child, Tatiana. That night after he had a chance to hold her, I asked him how he guessed. He said, "Sometimes God tells things to my brain and I just know it. I am one of His servants, but He serves me in a bigger way with His love."

I thought showers were reserved for brides and babies, but my friends in Denver had another idea in mind. First, my roommate Sarah Allen surprised me with a "book" shower, and her friends were gracious enough to give me at least fifty children's books for Lukas. Those included some of my favorites, "Where the Wild Things Are," "Goodnight Moon" and "The Grinch Who Stole Christmas."

Ben Martin, the teenage youth group leader at Colorado Community Church where I volunteered, surprised me with a second shower. I was inundated with blankets, more books, a bike, clothes and gifts that I hid from him and used for the next three Christmas holidays. I shared with them the story of his adoption and afterward they showered me with prayers for the trip ahead.

My friends from Denver, Julie Bayard, Deb Simon, and Erica Viviani hosted another shower, giving me everything from mattresses to sheets and comforters. My co-workers at Spalding—many who had secretly wanted me to bring home a child all along—gave me yet another shower. They blessed me with clothes, everything I needed for his room, and lots and lots of Legos—a very therapy-friendly gift, with gross and fine motor coordination skills always at the forefront. Little did I know then how fascinated Lukas would become with those little square Lego blocks that he fashioned into robots and ships and creatures for years to come.

When I got to California, my mom's friends, Carol Groseth and Hermien Cole, who had prayed about his adoption, hosted my last shower. I was not expecting any gifts from anyone; to say I was overwhelmed by these showers was an understatement. I received so many gifts for Lukas, I had more to hide away for a time when I needed them. When I prepared to bring him home, I realized that the only thing I would need were a couple of socks, and I was given a gift card for that. God truly provided everything I needed through the generosity of these incredible people.

CHAPTER 48

MY SON AT LAST

March 24, 2005—Age 9

We were at a church service just before Good Friday, and Lukas drew a picture of Jesus. He then said, "It doesn't matter if my picture of Jesus isn't perfect. He could look like a dot or a line because He is in everything."

My mom and I flew to Bucharest Romania on April 10, just after the "waiting period" I was given. Neither of us slept a wink that night on the plane. We landed at 2:00 p.m. We stayed at a hotel that didn't reflect the pretty price we paid. We were so exhausted that we fell asleep at 6:00 p.m. and slept the entire night until 6:00 a.m. the next morning. We flew later that next day into Oradea, which is one hour from Lukas' village in Marghita. We arrived in the evening and since the children at Casa Alba went to bed at 8:00 p.m., I was sure I wouldn't get to see Lukas until the next morning. I was hoping that Iorela would be the one to pick me up from the airport, as we had been walking through this process together.

My mom and I were making the much anticipated descent into Oradea and I gazed at my watch—it was 7:40 p.m. When we were about 2,000 feet from the ground—with my excitement mounting—I peered out of the window of the plane and saw a yellow vehicle. It was reminiscent of the Swedish van that Iorela sometimes drove, inching along below me. As the majority of the cars in Romania were red or white Dacia, this yellow van caught my attention. I jokingly quipped to my mom, "That could be Iorela coming to get us." Then I noticed that the van did not continue on the road past the airport, although I could not see if it had entered the parking lot.

I repeated, "Mom, I still don't see the van below us. It really could have stopped at the airport, and it might be Iorela. Maybe she has Gusztav with her."

My mom and I were some of the last people to get off of the plane. We walked toward the airport. I didn't realize it at the time, but Iorela informed me later that day that there was a barricade preventing people from going out onto the tarmac where the planes had landed. Lukas was small enough to fit right under the wooden barricade. Iorela said to the guard, "Can this boy go to meet his mother?" The guard answered sternly with a resounding "No." I still imagined that Lukas was asleep in bed and kept walking towards the airport.

Iorela noticed that the guard turned his gaze from Lukas, so she seized the moment and said to Lukas, "Run to her, Now!" Lukas squatted down under the post and darted his way to me. I saw a small child running to-wards me and I thought, "This can't be Lukas." But then that small child's image became clear. Lukas ran into my arms. As I held him, I couldn't hold back the tears. For someone who is not overly emotional, I think I cried more that year than all my years combined to date. Words cannot express what joy I felt in my spirit to hold my son for the first time not as someone else's, but as my own. My mom still regrets that she didn't have a video of our reunion to capture that magical moment.

Iorela also brought Gusztav to greet us at the airport, and we embraced them as mother and son for the first time as well. It was an incredible reunion. As we made our way back to Marghita, Lukas sat on my lap and held my hand, making sure not to let go. He asked me repeatedly for the one-hour car ride, "Where is the plane?" which I excitedly replied, "In Bucharest," happy to answer him over and over again, beginning my initiation into motherhood.

When we arrived at Casa Alba, and I tucked him in, we prayed for all of the children. Then he added, "Let's pray for Bunica," the name for grandma in Romania. It was incredible to hear him use this word for his new grandmother. He wondered why I had to stay at Herculane, now that I was his Mom. I tried to explain to him as best I could that we had to wait about ten more days until we were issued our immigration day in Bucharest. Although he was too young to really understand all of this, he didn't yet ask "Why?"

On April 12, several days after our fifteen-day waiting period was over, Iorela and I found out that the local judge would not let us leave the country yet. He wanted to "review" both of our documents that were already finalized and approved. We also found out that this was not legal, and he was not supposed to look back into records that were already processed. Yet he had a reputation for causing long, senseless delays. Within a few days, we were to hear if he decided to issue another fifteen-day waiting period. Ugh! I was starting to ask, "Why?"—wondering just what reasons were keeping me in Marghita longer than necessary, since all of the documents were finalized. This system, if one even existed, didn't seem to make any sense! Iorela and I both prayed that this judge would approve the papers.

The wonderful news arrived on April 19 that the judge re-approved Lukas' adoption. Our local social worker, Dan Bara, said, "Kristi's papers must have gone with God." He then mentioned, "Almost all of the other families' documents that were reviewed were denied approval by the judge, with Kristi and Lukas' as one of the few exceptions." Iorela then sadly informed me that her papers were denied. She cried with frustration since she would have to wait another fifteen days until she heard the judge's next decision. This was a time that I should have been celebrating, yet I couldn't truly celebrate when my heart ached for her. She had worked in this country for eight years—far longer than I—yet she was being held back by this one irrational judge.

Next, Lukas' passport had to be made, a process that could take a few weeks. Once in hand, we could set our appointment in Bucharest for immigration. It was unsettling to say the least that we didn't know any of the final dates this close to departure. The waiting was truly trying. Although I was thankful that my papers were approved, I still wondered why it was taking this long.

Shortly after I arrived, Lukas began to ask a question every day, several times a day, "Cand mergem cu avionul cu Lukas, si Kitty, si bunica," which meant, "When will we go by plane with Lukas, and Kristi and grandma?"

I didn't know the answer to this question, but I hoped we would soon find out.

When I arrived, I prayed that I would understand everything that Lukas said in Romanian. My understanding of the language was limited; I spoke in toddler-style or teen-slang Romanian, as I learned from the kids who surrounded me. When we finally found out that we could leave Marghita on May 1, since his passport had arrived, I realized my prayer was answered. I noticed during these last days that I understood everything Lukas said to me. The extra time that I had cursed and questioned every day actually gave me the ability to understand his fears, as well as his joys and his unending questions. Thank God that His plans are far better than mine!

We spent those days between Casa Alba and Herculane, walking up and down the streets, playing with several puppies that had just been born at Herculane, and watering the yard that he pretended to plow. On his final night at Casa Alba, we knelt by his bed, and he prayed for Laurentiu, Darius and Csaba, his roommates, Gusztav and Iorela, all of the other kids at Casa Alba, the puppies, and his new grandma, "bunica." I don't think he realized that he would be truly saying goodbye to them.

CHAPTER 49

SAYING GOODBYE TO ROMANIA

September 12, 2004—Age 8

Lukas and I went to Colorado to celebrate my niece Tatiana's baptism and to see my sister Julie, and her husband, Nicola Peccedi. Lukas had taken communion at the baptism at St. Patrick's in Telluride. Later that night when we were saying prayers, he asked, "Which part of Jesus' body did I take—His hands with the nail through it? Maybe even the rusty part. That shows what He did for us." I had taken communion before, and I had never tried to imagine what part of the body I was taking during the sacrament. His thoughts about Jesus' hands with the rusty nail led me to think about communion with even deeper reverence.

On our last full day there, Ligia—who had cared for Lukas since he was a baby—invited us to her family's house for dinner. We sat down to a feast that I will never forget. We ate meat that was the most tender that I have ever eaten, and we asked where they got it. They replied, "From our youngest calf." My mom and I sat next to each other and were so humbled that this family that lived with so little had given us a gift so great—their youngest and only calf. We both had to hold back the tears as we sat; I just squeezed her hand. She squeezed back—I knew she felt the same.

The last night at Herculane, the Swedes gave Lukas a goodbye dinner and Lars presented him with a Swedish flag that he swung proudly. I also gave him his first stuffed animal—a camel—given as a gift from my friend Scottie Hill Belfi. As he cried in his bunk, wondering why his roommates couldn't be with him, he clutched onto this camel as if it were his dearest friend. I packed his belongings, and it struck me that all he had to take to America from Casa Alba were two pair of pants and two shirts and his new camel. How different it was for me when I was four, with Fisher Price toys spewing out of our front porch, clothes to fill my dresser and closet, and more than a few stuffed animals to call my own. The camel was the only personal thing he had to take with him, and this didn't even come from Casa Alba, the place he called home.

The night before we flew into Bucharest, my mom received word from a woman named Nann Gonzalez. She was a volunteer from Maranatha Chapel in San Diego who worked with the orphans in that city. Nann had a room for volunteers that just happened to be available for us since there were no groups arriving until later that week. The hotels cost $200 per night, a fee I couldn't afford for two nights. We flew into Bucharest and found Nan, and met some of the children that she helped at the hospital where she volunteered. She helped to make the transition from Casa Alba to America more hospitable. Rather than being in a sterile hotel room, she gave us a homey environment. She also provided words of wisdom and encouragement during the Embassy appointments that had their own set of trials.

The next day, we met our translator and adoption facilitator, Vlad. Thank goodness for Vlad, who grew attached to Lukas in the two days that we were there. He ended up giving him piggyback rides from the U.S. Embassy to the doctor's appointments and back and forth to the passport office several times. I mentioned that we had Lukas' passport in hand. Well, the powers that be deemed it unacceptable during our last and final step before leaving the country. Why? Because Lukas was facing the camera. They explained to Vlad that his ear needed to be showing in the passport photo. So I ran alongside Vlad, Lukas on his shoulders, up and down the streets of Bucharest as we found a photo booth and ran back to the office with the happy photo.

Did I say happy? The Embassy rejected the passport photo again for just this reason. Lukas was smiling, and they didn't want to see his teeth; instead, they wanted to see his lips. He couldn't be smiling for the picture.

Well, at Casa Alba, he was told he was supposed to smile for photos, so he was very confused. I couldn't exactly explain this to him in my rustic style of the language, so Vlad came to the rescue. It took about five tries and then Vlad held Lukas' lips together and quickly ran out of the camera's eye, and the picture was captured. Lukas' lips were pursed like a sad child that had just finished eating sour grapes. We ran back to the Embassy, with time running out before the office closed for the day. The passport was finally accepted! We would finally get to leave the next day.

Vlad dropped us off at the airport and I truly was sad to say goodbye to him. Lukas was also sad to say goodbye to the man he considered his new friend. Before we stepped away from his car, he said, "Lukas is a very special boy!" In a short time he came to know what I also had discovered in Lukas when I first met him.

I walked inside and I excitedly thought to myself, "Has this time finally come? Am I really about to leave this country with my son?" As we prepared to go through the baggage check, a man in his sixties who had a stern expression—with wrinkles on his forehead that told me he scowled most of the time—approached Lukas and me. He was at least ten feet away from us when he began ranting something that I wish I wouldn't have heard, just minutes from getting on the plane. He spoke in Romanian, but I understood him clearly as my language skills had improved. He yelled, "How much did that boy cost—how much did you pay to steal him from our country?" I was startled and looked for an escape in case he started to accost me.

Lukas inched away from him and was closer to my mom, since he could sense by his tone that he wasn't being nice to me. I hoped that Lukas was too young to understand what he had said to me. I felt enraged for the first time and a wave of nausea swept over me. A part of me wanted to counter with something just as biting, asking him why he hadn't spent the last two years of his life thinking of and praying for this "boy." Instead I didn't say a word. I took a deep breath and I clutched Lukas' little hand that much tighter and swiftly walked through the security gate. I thought to myself, "I can't get on that plane fast enough." This was not the way I wanted to leave Romania—thinking of the caustic words of a cruel man.

Thankfully, Lukas' flight home was extraordinary from start to finish.

I remember the words of the Romanian woman next to me on the plane when she asked, "Did you hear what your child just said?" In my excitement, I told her I must have missed it.

She explained, "He just said, 'We are flying higher and higher. We must be getting closer to God.'" I sat back and marveled at his understanding at only four-and-a-half years of age, and the fact that he was now my son. I think that was the first time it really sunk in, as everything was touch-and-go until the last moment. I was thankful that this was the memory I would have leaving his country, of getting closer and closer to God. Looking back, when I first had the desire to go to Romania, Lukas was not yet born. I am so grateful that God closed the door when I originally wanted to go, so that the miracle of his adoption could take place.

November 30, 2000—Age 4

Lukas and I were flying home to Denver from Philadelphia, where we had just spent Thanksgiving with my friend, Sharon Okamoto, her sister Jodie, and her parents, Susanne and Ray. I had been able to share many of the parts of his adoption story with them, as Susanne had written a letter of recommendation for me to adopt Lukas. We sat on the plane next to a guy who was tattooed on every ounce of visible skin and with ear and lip piercings. During travel, I often found myself talking with the person next to me. Perhaps sharing Lukas' amazing story. I didn't know what to expect this time.

Lukas sat by the window and was drawing jagged lines in an upward slope. It looked like scribble, but I asked him what he was drawing. The guy next to me must have been curious too. Just loud enough for both of us to hear, Lukas said, "Jesus comes all the way down to get the people who died." When I asked about the jagged lines, he explained, "That is the way he comes down." Lukas continued to talk to me and the man next to me about God and heaven. When Lukas fell asleep, this man said he had been questioning his beliefs and didn't know what he thought about God. He was so surprised about what Lukas said, he told me he needed to start thinking about his own

faith. I hadn't anticipated a conversation of such depth. I saved
the drawing—scribbled on our travel brochure—and taped it
to my journal to remind me of those steps that lead to heaven.

He was filled with excitement and shrieked at times when he saw the clouds and the land below. He kept saying, "Avionul, Avionul," or "Plane, Plane," loud enough for everyone on the plane to hear. He was so thrilled to be traveling in the air. This was not an ordinary plane. It was a double-decker plane with a flight of stairs leading to first class and the cockpit. The flight attendants were so enamored by his raw emotions that they asked him if he wanted to go into the cockpit with the pilots. I wasn't invited, but he and camel were ushered in. The pilot gave him a banana that he enjoyed on the trip from Bucharest to Amsterdam.

He had never-ending questions about every detail of the plane—the luggage, the sky, the clouds, the passengers. You name it, he asked it. While on the plane, my mom helped to satisfy his need for movement by carrying him with outstretched arms, mimicking a plane. Lukas squealed with joy while he "flew" up and down the aisles for hours on end, but my mom and I wondered how many passengers were annoyed. To us it didn't matter, because he was certainly entertained. He did not cry or sleep for twenty hours until we flew from Minnesota for the last leg into San Diego. We were greeted at the airport by my sister, Julie, my dad, and our friends, Carolyn Hess, and Laurie and Katie Leasure, who I had known my entire life. They gave him a huge Winnie the Pooh balloon, which he carried with his camel all the way to my parents' house.

We spent a few wonderful weeks in San Diego, enjoying the warm weather and wonderful parks and zoos. While staying at my parents' house in Rancho Bernardo, I was wondering how much of the language he was beginning to understand. Someone let us borrow a toy car that he could drive and steer around my parents' house by pedaling with his feet. On the second day after he arrived in the states, my Dad set up a table and a pseudo-gate. He told Lukas that he could not pass through unless he had a ticket, which my Dad made from construction paper. My Dad thought that Lukas would do a couple laps around the house in that yellow and red car and would get bored of the activity. Instead, Lukas circled the house again and again for over an hour. Each time, he handed my dad the ticket, beaming ear to ear, waiting for permission to pass through the gate that my dad would open. Finally, my dad was the one who called it quits and said to Lukas, "The gate is closed!" Lukas quickly ran into the house and asked me, "What time does the gate open in the morning?" I told my Dad what he said and he shook his head, surprised by how quickly he was picking up the language.

While I was still in San Diego, my friend Heather Neely wanted to meet him. She had walked through Lukas' adoption journey with me and had encouraged me every step of the way. She and her husband Bryan flew down to San Diego from San Francisco, and we took him to see the ocean for the first time. My Dad insisted on joining us for the experience. I will never forget that day. He had never seen any body of water larger than a stream, let alone the ocean. When we got to Pacific Beach and he saw the water's wide expanse, he ripped off his T-shirt and ran into the waves, without an ounce of fear. I don't know if he had even heard of the word ocean before, and to witness his sheer joy as he jumped over the waves, laughing with delight, was a moment to remember. He looked at Heather and said, "This is like a giant bathtub!" Luckily, Bryan captured these moments on film.

Laurie Leasure, her husband Alan, and daughter Katie introduced us to the parks in San Diego, Lukas' first being Hilltop Park, near Carmel Mountain High School. Lukas, Katie and Alan entertained each other on the swings and slides and gave me a chance to sit and share the details of my last few weeks in Romania with Laurie. With its breathtaking views and wonderful winds, that park and the Leasure family ushered him into the U.S with a warm welcome.

September 1, 2003—Age 7

Lukas was in ankle deep water at the beach at Del Mar with my friends Erica and Holly. He said to Holly, "Won't it be neat when we get to heaven? We'll all be able to walk on water."

CHAPTER 50

CASA MEA?

May 8, 2005—Age 9

Lukas started talking about his thoughts about the world and heaven. He said, "If the world's like a house, heaven's the best room in the house. The baddest room is in the bottom where all the people that don't believe in God will be. If you go to heaven, angels carry you up steps above the first story (of the house). I think there are lots of gates in heaven, like seventeen gates of God's hand and eye. And there are twenty-eight shields and 1,000 angel guards by the gates." I had never talked to him about the gates of heaven, as I had only pictured one gate. Interestingly, the Bible does talk about angels in legions, or groups of 1,000. After he talked about multiple gates in heaven, I did some research. I found that in the Bible, in the book of Revelation, Chapter 21, verse 21, it mentioned that there were many gates in heaven. Again, when I asked him where he heard this he said, "God is saying it to my brain."

It was finally time for me to return to Denver. My Mom drove with Lukas and me, and we loaded into my car and started off on our sixteen-hour journey to what would be his new home. We didn't drive for more than an hour when he had to stop to go to the bathroom. We walked into the Shell Station, and he asked, "Casa mea?" I would have to tell him that no, this gladly was not his home. He would also ask this same question at the McDonald's.

We stopped to buy snacks at a small cafe in Utah with a store attached and walked inside—camel in tow—to find that the walls were mounted with the heads of deer, a bear, and an elk, along with some other dead animals. Their eyes were so piercing and the stiff beasts looked so alive, it was as if they could jump off of the wall and attack. Luckily, my Mom had learned a few words in Romanian, and she used one that came of good use that day, "Moritz, moritz," which means, "dead," to explain to him that the animals were dead. His face was still overcome with a look of horror as he asked again, "Casa Mea?" I told him, "No," once more. He was truly relieved, and he whispered to his camel not to worry, that this was not their home.

Lukas was so mesmerized as we drove past cars that towed boats, or campers or motorcycles—things he had never seen or heard about. With each new thing he would yell out with excitement and ask, "Chine's machina?" which I understood as, "Whose car is this?" He then wanted me to tell him all about it. An American flag was swinging in Colorado, and again he called out with such excitement. I wished he could share his newly acquired patriotic spirit with all Americans. Because of his mere wonder of discovering this whole new world, it was the most eye-opening road trip I had ever taken. Finally when we arrived in Denver at my apartment in the house on Humboldt Street, and he asked, "Casa Mea?" I could say, "Da" or "Yes."

CHAPTER 51

TRANSITIONAL CHALLENGES

Summer 2000—Age 4

Lukas and I were still in San Diego and were looking for a church. I had tried many that required highway driving. Lukas didn't want to go to church, partly because of his fear of the five-lane highways in San Diego. I said, "I think God wants us to go to church." He replied, "Jesus told me to stay right here." I listened, and we ended up finding Green Valley Church. It was about a mile away from my parents' home, and required no highway driving, something Lukas had needed.

There were so many transitions to life in America. While we lived in that house on Humboldt, Lukas woke me up three to four times a night. He typically slept through the night at Casa Alba, but he was afraid in his new surroundings. I slept on the couch on the same floor as his bedroom, rather than in the upstairs loft, so that he could find me easily. He would try not to startle me, but would stand nearby, and then tap me on the shoulder. He would ask questions like, "Are you going to send me back now?" and "Where are the other children at Casa Alba?" and "Why do the children at Casa Alba walk alone without mamas and papas?" These were the same questions I mentioned on the first page of this book; they were questions that were keeping him up at night at age four. They were questions that kept me up as well.

Not only was he afraid to sleep alone—without his three roommates— he was terrified of busy highways. Since his life in Romania had been confined mostly to the rooms at Casa Alba, he had not been on many car rides. He would scream with panic and hit his head against the back of the car seat so that I would stop the car due to his fear. Out of necessity I made an adjustment to take the side roads or two-lane streets, and tried to avoid highways as much as I could. Since my apartment was in a house bordering Cheesman Park, we walked in the park, played on the jungle gym there, and walked to *Lik's* for ice cream or to the grocery store to avoid the driving in the car as much as we could.

His fear of dogs was also quite clear, and not a mystery either. Lukas was raised to fear the street dogs. Other than the dog at Herculane and its puppies, he had a tremendous fear of the many dogs in Denver. He would climb upon my shoulders in a second whenever he saw a dog. It took a few months before he realized that these dogs were not wild strays, but were family pets. The dogs at Washington Park helped to teach him this. When we went to Wash Park to catch crayfish in the stream there—something I never would have known existed had I not had a child—the dogs were so well-trained that he learned that they would not bite him. I am thankful for all of those dog owners at the park for keeping their dogs on such good behavior. He was healed of dog-phobia because of them.

He also had a difficult time adjusting to warm food. Food from the hospital was cold by the time he ate it, so when warm food touched his lips, he would cry that it was burning him. In this moment, I was so thankful for my therapy background. While some people might have thought he was being dramatic, I deduced that since his sensory system hadn't experienced this warm temperature, it wasn't ready to receive warm input. I learned to put ice in his soup and give him cold toast for the next few years. His bath water also had to be tepid or it felt like it was burning him.

Yet another sensory issue was touch. Again, as he had not been held as an infant as often as most children, he was hypersensitive to light touch. If I accidently touched him with a fingernail, he would feel as if I was cutting him with a the blade of a knife. Again, I was thankful for what I learned in PT school about our sensory systems, as it allowed me to understand the issues that were difficult for him and to adapt to his needs.

Thankfully, language wasn't one of his difficult hurdles. He was fluent in English about three months after his arrival. His preschool teacher, Mrs.

Cooper, told her class that they would be getting a new kid in the classroom and that they would need to teach him English. After the first day, she told my mom, "The other children didn't need to teach him a thing. I think he will be teaching them."

He spoke so well by the time he entered Kindergarten, Miss O'Beirne, could not tell that he had ever spoken another language. He learned the language quickly but wasn't quite ready to make the transition in other areas. He called me "Kitty" for a long time, and I wondered when he would acquire the word "Mama." Maybe he couldn't trust that word. I waited until he was ready to use this powerful word—it would take him about six months.

Summer 2001—Age 5

Lukas was staring into my eyes and then he announced, "The light comes into the black part. I know that's how you see. It's the black part that helps you see." I never explained how the eye worked, but he was a curious boy and always tried to figure out how things worked. I don't think I figured out how the eye worked until ninth grade biology class.

CHAPTER 52

FOURTH OF JULY TO REMEMBER

Before I went back to work, Lukas and I made a trip to D.C. to see my college friends, Mahri Aste, Tory Robinson Mackey and Sandi Dollar Shriner. At the time, Mahri was an elementary school teacher. She anticipated that Lukas would have some language difficulties, or would still be speaking Romanian, since he had only been in the states for two months. She was surprised when he opened the bug collection kit she and her family had given him, and he said in clear English, "Will the bugs stay alive if I catch them and put them in here?" She laughed and commented that he was picking up English faster than some of her students that had been in the states for a year.

Tory brought a few bags full of boys clothes that her sister Kate's sons could no longer wear. Tory and her sister were known for their fun sense of style, so I must say that his wardrobe was quite complete, not to mention fashion-friendly. Sandi also surprised me with gifts and clothes for Lukas to wear. I was amazed that I wouldn't need to spend a dime on clothes or toys—a dime I really couldn't spare.

Mahri, Lukas and I celebrated the Fourth of July in D.C, and decided to sit just yards away from the Washington Monument for the fireworks. I won't fail to mention that this was the year 2000, and we were in the nation's capital. We would be watching the biggest fireworks display of the new millennium—most likely the biggest in the U.S. The big show started to light up the sky, and at first, I thought we would need to leave immediately. Lukas was scared for his life, and had no idea what that booming noise was, let alone the colors lighting up the sky. I am sure many other kids have the same response. Being a veteran with kids, Mahri told me to cover his ears. That was the trick. He sat there mesmerized, looking up at the sky. I was just as mesmerized, but for a different reason. Patriotic songs were humming on radios in cars nearby, and I almost could not believe that I was sitting in the capitol, with my new son, watching fireworks, in a land that he would now call home.

November 2, 2003—Age 7

Lukas said to me one day, "Do you know why God put the sun so far away? If it was any closer, it would burn us like fried bacon." I was never more thankful for the placement of the sun.

CHAPTER 53

Precious Gift

While on the East coast, Lukas and I made our way to Baltimore for the wedding of my friend Sharon Leilich to Ken Hollis. Mahri's dad George let us borrow his car, and he warned me about the D.C. traffic and told me to look out for the H.O.V. lane to save time. I remember driving with Lukas sitting just in back of me in his car seat. I was fairly new to the experience of driving with a child. As I flew past the other drivers who seemed to be cursing at me and giving me the bird, I couldn't figure out if or why I was the target of road rage. As Lukas and I sailed along in George's Lincoln Continental, passing all of the frustrated people stuck in traffic, the fourth driver passed me, yelling through the window that I should be in the other lane. Finally it dawned on me. Lukas was so small that his booster seat didn't quite boost him high enough to be seen by those behind the wheel. The hostile drivers thought I was violating the H.O.V. carpool rules, driving alone, and avoiding the sluggish traffic that maddened them. With middle fingers waving at me all the way to Baltimore, I imagined pushing Lukas in a stroller in Romania as a horse and buggy passed by, and I thought to myself, "Welcome to the U.S.A, Lukas!"

Thankfully we made it to Baltimore for Sharon's wedding without being run off of the beltway. This ceremony would be a new experience for Lukas as he was asked to be a ring-bearer and I was asked to be a bridesmaid. Before the wedding, Sharon gave gifts to everyone in the wedding party, including Lukas. All of the women immediately opened their gifts, but I noticed Lukas just held onto his. It was time to leave her apartment and drive to the church. As we walked to the car, Lukas clutched his gift carefully with his pudgy little fingers. While in the car, Sharon noticed that Lukas still sat with his gift, unopened on his lap. She asked him if he wanted to open it, and he said, "No." Two times a year, on his birthday and Christmas, he received one gift that was usually taken by someone else, or broken within minutes. He whispered to me in Romanian that he was so excited that he wanted to hold it for a little while. Lukas still carried the box tightly as we walked up the steps to the church. He didn't open it until we were ready to leave for Denver.

We returned to Denver and a longtime friend from my pre-school years, Jean Oxendine Plaschke, came to meet the newest addition to my family. She brought with her an entire suitcase of boys' clothes, hand-me-downs from one of her cousins, and in sizes from aged four to eight. I don't think I needed to shop for clothes until he was almost eight! We then visited local parks and introduced him to playgrounds throughout Denver.

Next, my cousin Todd Hawkins and his wife-to-be, Silvia, arrived from Indiana. I remember Lukas' first trip to the mountains in Estes National Park with Todd and Silvia. I witnessed Lukas sitting on Silvia's lap for over thirty minutes as he inspected a wandering ant that crawled on Silvia's hand and then onto his. He seemed enthralled, and content to sit and absorb the beauty of nature that unfolded before him. We drove to one mountain peak and were above 10,000 ft. It was July, and hovering around ninety sweltering degrees in Denver. But in the mountains of Colorado—in winter or in summer—I learned to be prepared for extremes when it came to weather. We climbed some of the rocks at the peak and the snow began to fall. I ran to the car and wrapped my bulky green sweater around Lukas' head. As the snowflakes danced on his cheeks and eyelashes, he ran toward Todd and Silvia, his arms stretched toward the sky. I will never forget his smile at that moment, one that radiated the joy he felt—no words were needed to understand his exhilaration. We were all grateful for that Rocky Mountain high!

Todd and Silvia continued their travels West, and I knew that in a few days, my leave of absence from work was about to come to end. I found it hard to imagine returning to work in a few weeks, while trying to settle in as a new mom. I was soon to find out.

Summer 2001—Age 5

My mom's cat, Minka, was killed by a coyote. Unfortunately, my mom and I witnessed it when it was too late to rescue her, which made it that much more traumatizing. I decided that it would be too upsetting to tell Lukas exactly what happened, but I explained to him the next morning that he wouldn't be seeing Minka anymore as she had died. He asked me how it happened and then asked, "Was it a mountain liner?," meaning a mountain lion. I was glad that I could say it was not a mountain lion. He barraged me with questions, but I just said she was gone. He said, "Well, if you aren't going to tell me, God will tell me tonight because I need to know." I slept on that thought. He hadn't talked to my parents or anyone else about it, and when he woke the next morning he announced, "I need to write a letter to Nika." (He had shortened the Romanian name for grandma from bunica to "Nika.")

As he still couldn't write, I got out my pen and was ready to write what he had to say to his grandmother. His letter read, "Dear Nika, I know that you are sad and I am sad, too. But God told me that the coyotes needed Minka for her meat. So please don't be sad. These are my words, Lukas." I knew I was the only one who had talked to him about the cat dying and I hadn't mentioned coyotes, so I had to conclude that God did talk to him about the cat being killed by hungry coyotes. He then asked me, "How did Minka get to heaven?" I paused for a second and then he said, "I know, God took Minka to heaven in a cat chariot!" He gave his letter to my mom, and she and I agreed that the image of Minka in that cat chariot on her way to heaven eased the sadness that we were feeling and left us both with a smile.

CHAPTER 54

BACK TO BASICS

y friend Julie Bayard offered to make my transition back to work more bearable. Before I left to bring him home, she asked me if I would like her to watch him while I was at work. She was an occupational therapist, and understood sensory challenges perhaps better than I did. Having her care for him during the day was a true blessing. In addition, my friend, Erica Viviana, came to my apartment almost every night after work to help me cook, wash dishes or entertain Lukas. She would also help me with any extra housework so that I could get him ready for bed. I was working ten-hour days, and sometimes left at the house at 6:30 a.m. and returned home from work at 6:30 p.m., so the help that she gave to me was treasured. She also let us use the pool at her apartment that first summer, where he learned to swim.

One sweet reunion in Denver was with the Brown family. Courtney Brown lived in Golden, Colorado, but I first met her as she was volunteering at Casa Alba when my Mom and I went to bring Lukas home from Romania. Courtney's father had taken her to volunteer at the hospital with orphaned children when she was only sixteen. So Courtney held Lukas when he first arrived at the hospital, before there was an opening for him to be transferred to Casa Alba. Lukas and I went to visit the Brown family, and they took us out on their boat. We shared in a wonderful dinner, visiting their six girls, including Courtney.

What amazed me about this visit was that while sitting on a bench—just after we stepped off of the boat—I mentioned that I had to prepare a poster of Lukas' childhood pictures for his preschool class in Denver. He was "student of the week," and Lukas insisted, "I need to have baby pictures. The teacher told me to make sure it has baby pictures." What was I going to do? I had taken many pictures—being that this was one of my hobbies—but how was I going to get baby pictures for his class on Monday, the next day? I told Courtney about my dilemma. She said with excitement, "I think we have baby pictures of Lukas. When I was sixteen, I held Lukas when he was a baby at the hospital, and I think my dad took a few pictures of me holding him." I couldn't believe it. But then nothing was beyond belief when it came to his needs. When we got back to her house, she found baby pictures of Lukas—the day before he needed them for his class presentation. I sensed divine intervention at work.

CHAPTER 55

MOVING ON

March 18, 2003—Age 7

While saying prayers, Lukas asked, "Mama, can we pray for a daddy?" In my mind I really wasn't feeling ready, even though I always wanted to get married. But I prayed, "God, send us a daddy when I am ready." He said, "Stop, Mom, that's not the right prayer. Mama, you are ready. Pray He sends one when He chooses."

Shortly after returning to work at Spalding, I realized that I could not work ten-hour days and do the best as a mom to help Lukas make all the adjustments he needed. I talked to my sister, Julie, and she said that she thought I needed to move to San Diego to be closer to our family. After working six months, I decided that my family could provide that village of support that he needed. I resigned from Spalding and surprised my parents with a Christmas gift they were hoping for—our move to San Diego.

Julie came from San Diego to help me with the move. Lukas was attached at my hip and wouldn't let me out of his sight to pack a box. At the last minute, Julie and I realized we needed help. My mom came to our rescue and was on the next plane to Denver to help with the packing process. The teens from my youth group—sent by the leader, Ben Martin—came to load all of the boxes onto the U-Haul truck that my sister, Julie, would drive to San Diego for me. My friends Deb, Thomas Simon and Mark Chase packed every last box onto the truck, and into my car. I was ready to say goodbye to the city I had known for a decade, with my Mom in my car, and Lukas with Julie in the big truck. It was no surprise that he just had to be in that big truck.

Just before we pulled away, a youth group volunteer named Tod Muller arrived. He was carrying something rectangular in his hands. He wanted me to open it in front of him. I really didn't know if I could squeeze one more thing into my car. I opened his gift and was in awe. He had painted a portrait of Lukas that was as close to a perfect replica as I could imagine. He completely surprised me as he told me that he had to take photos of children for his art class. I didn't think anything of it. The portrait pictured Lukas just after he had arrived from Romania, holding up four fingers to show his age. I made sure to make room for it in my car. This precious gift has hung in a special place in every house I have lived in since that move. It will always remind me of the fragile age and time when he arrived.

Interestingly, within two nights of settling into my parents house in Rancho Bernardo, Lukas knew he was surrounded by a family that loved him, and he no longer woke me three to four times a night to ask questions about being sent back to Romania. He slept through the night every night after that.

I found out several months after his arrival in the States that Romania closed its doors to international adoption. This meant that married couples and single women, including anyone in any country other than Romania, could no longer adopt a child from that country. Just months after Lukas was able to walk through that door, it was shut. I was struck by the timing and how I had a sense of urgency in my heart. I never would have completed his adoption packet in five days had God not been whispering to me to move quickly.

July 2001—Age 5

My cousin, Todd Hawkins, and his girlfriend, Silvia, were visiting us in San Diego. Todd was sitting outside as Lukas worked on one of his drawings. Todd came in and showed me the picture, with an element of mystery in his voice. He said, "Lukas drew a picture of you." I took a look but I couldn't really discern the action of the images. Todd explained to me how

Lukas interpreted the picture and said, "Lukas drew a picture of you, Papa and Bunica (grandma), ascending out of rock tombs into the heavens, surrounded by angels." Todd thought of this as a bit unusual for a young child, and I told him that I hadn't been telling him about rock tombs lately. This would be his first family portrait.

CHAPTER 56

WHAT GOD HAS SPOKEN TO THE CHILD

May 2, 2004—Age 8

Lukas was getting ready for bed and he said, "After Eve, a dark sin cloud came over the earth. When Jesus died, a white cloud came to the earth." I asked him again where he had heard that and he responded, "God is speaking it to my brain."

Lukas had no idea when I first adopted him at age four that I felt his story was so incredible that I thought I had to write about it. Some people tried to dissuade me from writing in order to protect Lukas and his privacy. Yet I was so convinced that I was to write all of the miracles that God had performed to complete this adoption that I shared it with my pastor, Doug Kyle, at Green Valley Church. At the time, Lukas had just turned five. I told Doug that something seemed to hold me back from writing. He spoke these words of wisdom: "Maybe the story isn't finished yet?"

When Lukas was eleven, we were driving down Pomerado Road in San Diego when Lukas said, "It is time, Mama." I asked curiously, "Time for what?" He answered without hesitating, "Time to write the book—what God has spoken to the child." I knew then that the time had come for me to write the story. He had given me permission to write the story—the entire story.

I weaved most of his sayings throughout the story, but I couldn't find a place where the next three quotes seemed to fit. I include them here and I add them with the knowledge that some may be offended by reading them. As a mother, I was startled when he told me these things as an eleven-year-old. They are rather compelling, and a part of me would have felt more "comfortable" not including them. But, when I reflected on that car ride when Lukas told me that I had to write the book, he also said we needed to write it because "there is a war on faith and people need to understand who God is." I knew then that I needed to tell the whole story, even if parts were "uncomfortable" for me, and perhaps, for those who read them.

July 2007—Age 11

My cousin was getting married in South Carolina, and my college roommate, Tory Robinson Mackey just so happened to live in Pawley's Island, close to the wedding site. Lukas had gone through an especially rough year of sickness, stemming from an intestinal infection and illness that he developed in Romania. It persisted for years and lead to severe abdominal distress that would cause heartburn and chest pain, and at times a resultant feeling of anxiety. After a wonderful day at the beach with Tory and her kids, Jed and Hannan, his stomach issues reared their ugly head again. Later that night, as tears rolled down his cheeks, he said, "I feel like a snake is wrapping itself around my neck and it is trying to squeeze my Jesus out of me." He had never heard of the analogy of the serpent with the "dark side," but he was describing this for me, and seemed to express that the physical battle that he was going through also felt like a spiritual battle of sorts.

June 1, 2007—Age 11

Lukas was sitting in his room and he said, "I had a vision while I was awake. The souls go down to the boiling pot and the souls are dumped in, then they float and dissolve into nothing. You don't exist, you wasted yourself, your life is over, your soul is gone. You have a decision—go to heaven, have eternal life, or go to hell, have no life, no future. When souls die, the demons laugh each time a soul disappears into oblivion." He said to me insistently, "We have to tell people, Mom! They have to know! They have to know who God is and that He loves them."

July 2007—Age 11

Lukas and I went to see Akiane's art exhibit in San Diego. She is a prodigy in art and poetry who began drawing and painting when she was four and has been featured on Oprah and 20/20. Each of her paintings usually has an interpretation, and she posted this beside her paintings at the show. Lukas was eleven and he was sitting on a bench about twenty feet from one of her paintings. He didn't go up to read any of the interpretations due to his dyslexia, but just looked at them from a distance. He didn't know that she did not have an interpretation for one of her paintings that had pyramids with waves crashing into them.

Lukas said to me, "I have seen this same image in my dreams. I have seen it a few times. God is telling me that the picture is about the end of the world as we know it. The pyramids show the earth. The water is coming over part of the earth at the end of the world. The bubbles that are floating up are the souls going to heaven." Lukas didn't know that Akiane believed that God gave her these images and gave her the meaning behind them, except this painting. Upon reading her symbolic interpretations, I did notice that she had another painting with bubbles rising in the sky and she said that these bubbles represented the souls of people. I hope to contact her to explain what Lukas thought God told him about that image.

PART II

CHAPTER 57

RETURN TO ROMANIA

February 10, 2009—Age 13

Lukas was sitting on his bed and he said to me, "I haven't been hearing from God as often. Maybe because there are so many distractions and things like video games. God is saying to see with your heart and not your eyes. Also, do not listen to the ones around you, but to the one, true God. He is telling me there is no need to worry, angels are all around you and that's the best comfort of all."

Lukas and I finally decided to return to his village of Marghita, Romania, about three years ago. Neither of us had set foot in Romania for thirteen years. He was then seventeen years old. I called Iorela in Sweden and asked if she wanted to join us, and she said, "Gusztav and I were already planning on going." Lukas and I decided to meet them in Marghita so that Lukas could see where he had grown up for those first four years. The night before we left, Lukas and I were eating at a restaurant. He said to me, "I wonder if everyone here had their faces painted to represent the color of their country, would I see anyone from Romania? I just need to see the color of my people."

We took the voyage. We were in a state of delirium when we landed in Budapest, eager for the taxi that would take us directly to his village. That four-hour taxi ride became a whole lot longer as our taxi driver was waiting for someone to join us. We waited in the parking lot—and in a few other parking lots next to dilapidated old planes—for hours in the hot sun. When I asked him how much longer we needed to wait, he kept saying, "Ten minutes, ten minutes" for the next four hours. We would circle around the airport lot, and just when I would think that we were heading out of the airport, I would realize the driver was circling around once again. That someone that we were waiting for was a wonderful guy named Trevor from North Carolina, who was going to build in a poor village near Oradea—an hour from Lukas' birthplace. We had never met this guy until he ended up in our taxi.

We were delayed at the border between Hungary and Romania, but Trevor thought that offering gummy bears to the border patrol might expedite the process. Unfortunately, the border patrol did not accept this type of offer, nor did he find humor in this. I thought we might be detained there for hours. Thankfully, after a brief thirty-minute wait, we were finally granted entrance into Romania.

The taxi driver told us that we had arrived in Oradea, and he was about to leave Trevor at the wrong destination. It would have been difficult to locate his contact in the village due to cell phone issues. Trevor said, "I think this is it." I knew that it was not, as it was a ramshackle hut, rather than a volunteer house. I knew that we were not in the right section of town. The taxi driver wanted Trevor to get out. I could sense that he was irritated that we were in the "gypsy" section of town. I insisted that the driver wait so that we could take Trevor to his destination.

We stood near a very poor house with ten gypsy children running around us as we tried to figure out where to find his contact. I noticed that Lukas did not waste any time getting to know the locals. I saw him racing up and down the street with the children. He tried to speak with some of them, and told them that he lived in America, but was from Romania. I was able to find some people who understood my broken Romanian, as Trevor didn't know the language. Finally, I found a man—who just so happened to be gypsy—who knew the contact that Trevor was looking for, and he led us directly by bicycle to the mission house, Children of the Son. If we hadn't been in that taxi, and demanded that the taxi driver wait until we found Trevor's contact, it may have taken him several more anxious hours to find his way. After getting his contact information, we said goodbye to him. I told him that I might call him someday in the States and return with him to that village to build homes or schools for the people in that small town. We would just have to find a different taxi driver.

Lukas and I got in the car, and his excitement was evident. But he could also sense the tension that the taxi driver had during our last encounter with the locals. He whispered to me, so that the driver couldn't hear us," Mom, why did he have such a bad attitude and act so rude—we were just trying to help Trevor?"

I answered him very succinctly and quietly, "He didn't want to be in that area of town." The social clashes were too sensitive an issue to discuss on two hours of sleep, especially with the taxi driver in ear-shot. I had visions of him leaving us in a sunflower field if we mentioned anything else that irritated him. And I desperately wanted to make it safely to Marghita.

Lukas commented, "Mom, these people look like me—their skin, their hair, their eyes. Why are we not going to be staying here longer? I can already tell that the time here will not be long enough."

December 13, 2006—Age 11

Lukas was brushing his teeth, looking in the mirror and he said to me, "I'm not sure mirrors were a good invention. With mirrors, we know to be critical about ourselves. If we didn't have mirrors, we wouldn't know if we were beautiful or ugly. We would just live by who we are inside. Now, it seems like everything is set on appearances. So I'm not sure how I feel about mirrors."

CHAPTER 58

SWEET REUNION

July 5, 2006—Age 10

Lukas woke up one morning and said, "I had a dream last night that I went to Romania and saw Lars (the orphan's foundation director). Then someone gave me a gift, something I couldn't use. And they gave me a piece of paper, and I said, 'Thank you, thank you.'" Lukas continued to say, "I am not really sure what this dream or the piece of paper meant, mom." This piqued my interest in returning to Romania with Lukas to reunite with Lars and many of the Romanians who rescued so many of the children, including my son. I wondered who might give him this piece of paper as a gift. I hoped we would find out one day.

The taxi driver finally found the new "Herculane" or Swedish volunteer house in Marghita—even if five hours behind schedule. The first to greet us were Iorela and Gusztav, and had an incredible reunion with them. They had traveled to the U.S. to see us twice before, and we had been to Sweden to see them as well. It had been five years since we had last seen them in the States. We were more than excited to see them again. Who else was there to greet us but Lars, still working there after perhaps twenty years. It was overwhelming for all of us. My friend Courtney Brown, who held Lukas at the hospital orphanage as a baby when she was only sixteen, also greeted us. She was the friend from Denver who had baby pictures of Lukas, just when he needed them for preschool class. She met and married a Swede while there and she continued the volunteer work she had done for about a decade.

One of Lukas' main desires was to see his half-sister Silvia. She was nineteen, and had never been adopted due to severe autism. I asked Lukas what he remembered most about Silvia and he replied, "I can just picture her eating the paint chips from the walls or the metal heaters." I shuddered at this memory and hoped that their reunion would be a good one.

Iorela knew that Lukas was eager to see her. Shortly after we woke up the next morning, she told us we would go to see Silvia. Iorela, Gusztav, Lukas, and I walked down the same cobblestone streets—which I had walked along so many times before— and passed horses drawing buggies behind them, just as they had done thirteen years ago. I brought my camera and told Lukas to take pictures of anything that caught his eye. He stopped at a church that I remembered passing with him in a stroller, many years ago. I looked at the church with its long white steeple, and a feeling of thankfulness swept over me. I stood here now with Lukas as my son.

We continued walking. We finally came to the house where Silvia lived with a few other children who were disabled and considered unadoptable. Iorela had explained to me years ago that Silvia desperately wanted a home to call her own, and that she was aware that other children from Casa Alba had found homes and families. Lars and the other foundation members came up with a solution. They raised enough money and bought a house that they dedicated to Lukas' sister, and called it Casa Silvia. The Swedes knew that otherwise she and the other children would have been sent to a state institution.

We climbed the stairs and were greeted by a woman named Lidia Micula, whom I knew from my volunteer work at Casa Alba. She was an amazing woman from Marghita who became the director of Casa Alba after Iorela moved back to Sweden with Gusztav. She now worked as the director and also a house mother for Casa Silvia. She had extensively studied in Romania and in the U.S. about children who suffered from abandonment and abuse and learned many interventions to try to best help them. She called Silvia to the door and Silvia's eyes lit up with excitement. She had been praying to see Lukas and didn't know that he was coming. When she saw him, she knew immediately who it was. They embraced, and she held onto him as if she would never let him go. Because she had difficulty speaking, she made him a card on a simple piece of paper with floral decorations on it and gave it to him. He said, "Thank you, thank you."

Just then, it hit me! I remembered Lukas' dream that I mentioned previously in the text from July 5, 2006, in which he dreamt that he went back to Romania and saw Lars, and then someone gave him a gift of a piece of paper and he had the same response, "Thank you, thank you," not knowing what this meant. Now seven years later, it was clear that his dream had been realized. His meeting with Silvia was nothing short of magical.

We all walked outside into a yard with a play area, a bench and a swing. I looked over near the bench and recognized Lavinia, one of Lukas' roommates at Casa Alba at one time. She was the little girl with eyes as big as saucers who could not stand or walk when I began working with her at age two. I watched her take her first steps when she was almost four years old. She was also a teenager now. Even though she was delayed mentally and could not verbally communicate, she smiled when she saw us. She also waved her hands in the air and looked off at an angle, not making eye contact. But she had a smile on her face that told me she was familiar with me. She walked in the green grass with a calm nature that reflected the fact that she now had a home.

We visited with Silvia and the other children for a few hours. She showed us her room and I noticed that she did not have any photographs beside her bed. I knew then the gift that we would get for her. We walked into the town that now had a few gift shops and found a picture frame for her. When we returned later that week, we told her that we would send a photo of her with Lukas that she could put in that frame. She beamed from ear to ear. I told her that she would be a part of our family in spirit, even though we would be miles apart.

I remembered a time when she was four, and she cried for hours through the night, but she could not speak. Although she repeated herself at times in an echolalic way, she could tell Lukas that she loved him, prayed for him, and thought about him while he was in America. I was amazed at the progress she had made due to the persistence, care, and love from the volunteers from Romania, Sweden, and other countries. Lukas told me later that the time with Silvia was one of the highlights of his trip.

CHAPTER 59

RETURN TO CASA ALBA

February 2008—Age 12

I had just decided to take Lukas out of public school as he was struggling due to dyslexia. The school would not make the accommodations needed for him to succeed when he was in fifth grade. He was so upset about school that he drew a picture for me of a heart with dagger marks cut through it. When I asked him about the drawing, he said, "School is killing my soul and stealing my joy." He asked me to homeschool him for this reason.

Thankfully, I had researched home-schools and charter schools, and I found what was the perfect fit in Dehesa Charter School that included some classes with other students, and other at-home studies. While I was driving him to an art class provided by Dehesa, he looked up to a hillside that had recently been charred and blackened by the October firestorm of 2007. This fire left hundreds in our town without homes. He said, "Look at the hill, Mom. I see a patch of green on the dark hill. God is showing me that just as He will rebuild the green on the darkened hillside, he will lift me up out of the pit of sadness and depression. He will not leave us with only the memory of the fire."

The next day, Iorela told me that she was given keys to Casa Alba and that we were given permission to see inside. Lukas, Gusztav, Iorela and I walked to Casa Alba. When we stepped inside the building, I didn't know how much Lukas would remember. He walked up the steps, through the door, and directly to his room and said, "This was my room, wasn't it?" I told him, "Yes, it was." It was hard to believe he remembered it, as he hadn't seen it since he was four years old.

We walked throughout the building and into each room where he played or napped or ate. Then we walked outside, and he and Gusztav sat on a rusty white swing that they had swung on thirteen years prior. Two old metal rings swung from a bar that sat too high for any of the children to use, as if they had been abandoned, too. We walked past the building that had crusty iron bars over the windows, and chipped, white paint falling from the door. A broken lamp dangled above the door, no longer providing light to people coming or going.

I walked next to the metal fence that guided our way to the entrance gate, and noticed an old, white wooden cross on the opposing wall. It was visible through a gaping hole in the torn, twisted pieces of metal. I thought of the picture this painted of life and hope—despite the broken, mangled wire that tried to hold the children in its grip. A part of me almost couldn't believe that these boys had once lived here and now had become our sons. The gate to so many doors had to open for both of us to call these boys our own.

The next day I had a special reunion with my friend Brenda Jackson from Colorado. Yes, I was in Romania, but I met Brenda while working at Spalding Rehab Hospital, as she was also a therapist. She called me one day while she was overseas, asking me for the contact number in Romania so that she could do volunteer work there. I told her it was quite difficult to contact someone at the volunteer house who could help her fulfill her desires, but I kept my fingers crossed.

She somehow got in touch with Lars and his wife Barbro. That was in 2002. It was now 2013. She had volunteered there ever since. First, she had been the house mother for Lukas' sister and the other girls at Casa Silvia. I was amazed that one of my friends was actually caring for my son's half-sister—it was hard to comprehend.

Iorela, Gusztav, Lukas and I went to her home and met a boy named Alex that she was trying to adopt. There were different rules for adoption if you resided in Romania, as she now did. She was also caring for a girl with autism, and housed a young teenage girl with a baby. The teenager wouldn't have been able to keep her baby unless Brenda housed them both. Previously, Brenda had cared for three children whose mother was sick and dying from cancer. I could tell that Brenda had her hands full, but also that she was doing incredible work here.

We also found Ligia, the woman who cared for Lukas at Casa Alba, and who would have loved to adopt Lukas but couldn't because she was too young at the time and had poor health. When we both found her, she and I couldn't hold back the tears. She held Lukas with the warmest embrace, which he returned. I talked to her for several hours while Lukas played soccer with the teenage orphans in a gym built by Lars and the children's foundation. I truly was so amazed at how the foundation still provided for these children in even better ways. I was also amazed at the miracle that Lukas was my son and wouldn't have to live without family for the rest of his life, like many of the teens we met that day.

During the soccer game, we recognized some of the American volunteers that we knew from Denver, the Deweys. Fred and Karleen Dewey had spent years leading camps in the Black Forest for the orphans in the area. Now their son Scott Dewey and his wife Melanie volunteered in Marghita trying to further the cause. Scott and I kept in touch when he was back in Denver and he sent me updates about their work in Marghita throughout the years. Lukas and I were able to go to his apartment and meet Melanie, their sons, and some teens that they assisted in that town—teens that had no home after the orphanage.

One of those teens was Craciun, a roommate of Lukas' when Lukas was a toddler. Although they had distant memories of each other, I remembered Craciun fondly. He was one of the boys I cared for from time to time and I knew him to be such a sweet, quiet boy. The Deweys had taken Craciun in as part of their family. Although he was too old to be legally adopted by them, they considered him to be their son. It was wonderful to see that that boy I had known as a shy, timid toddler now had a family of his own.

CHAPTER 60

FRUIT FROM BARREN TREES

August 1, 2009—Age 13

I was looking at the journal I kept of Lukas' sayings, and I wanted to know if he remembered the image he had of the tree. He said, "Yes, I remember." I asked him, "Did you say that God was in the tree?," and he replied, "No, God is the tree. The leaves are the people." He went on to explain this image in more detail. He said, "When you lose faith in God, you fall off the tree. Your faith has been lost. New leaves that grow are souls that find faith. There are always souls that can come back, find their faith. They can be regrown, and acorns fall off, and new life can grow again. In autumn, the tree loses all the leaves. It is representing the new souls that go to heaven. New souls can grow as they gain faith." I wasn't sure if he had remembered this, as it had been four years since he told me the first time. I was surprised that he remembered it quite clearly, and with more details and insight. Interestingly, the Bible, in Genesis 3:24, speaks of the angels in the Garden of Eden guarding the tree of life.

Lars was able to show me the work the foundation had done in the thirteen years since I had been there. He and the foundation had amazingly raised funds to build an apartment building that housed up to twenty teenagers. If not for that shelter, they would have been homeless.

What happened to the orphans after they became eighteen and no longer in an orphanage and cared for by their country? They found themselves on the streets without a home. Many gravitated towards a life filled with drugs, prostitution, crime, homelessness and hopelessness unless they were one of the few who could find work. Many did not have life skills to care for themselves, let alone to find a job.

As I walked toward the yellow apartment building on the same hillside as the apple trees that I had walked past every day many years ago, a thought came to me. Thirteen years ago, I had heard God's voice saying He was caring for these orphans like tending to the barren trees in winter time. And now, I stood before a new home that housed and provided for twenty of those children. I was in awe. That yellow house—a color common for Swedish homes but not often used for homes in Marghita—was a symbol of the work the Swedish people had done in this town. It stood on that hillside as a beacon of hope.

If this wasn't enough, Lars had built a comprehensive volunteer headquarters that was beyond my imagination. It housed a large warehouse depot for goods for the children still abandoned. The grounds included a carwash, and a car repair area where the young men learned to fix or wash cars and gain employment in an area where they otherwise would have trouble finding work. Office space for Lars and for foundation meetings, and a volunteer house with an Ikea-like style was also built by the foundation on this land. It had one amazing feature—hot running water at any time of the day! It was a far cry from the volunteer house named "Herculane" I had lived in when I worked there.

Lukas, Gusztav, Iorela and I were able to take a tour of the town as well. One incredible thing that I noticed immediately was that there was now a grocery store. It had bottled water! I walked up and down the aisles, finding "Nutella" and "Cheerios" and almost couldn't believe I was in the same town. I was thankful that people here no longer had to go to several stores just to prepare a meal and that they had a diversity of fruits and vegetables at their fingertips.

I had one desire while in this village—that was to photograph the sunflowers. Photography was something I enjoyed, and the sunflowers in Romania were prolific. One morning Lars and Barbro's daughter,

Sofia—who had lived in this village and sacrificed for the children along with her parents for more than twenty years—offered to take me to see the sunflower fields. We walked in rows and rows of sunflowers that stood taller than my five-foot-three-inch frame. They stood in fields as far as the eye could see. Since I spent most of my time in Romania in winter and fall, witnessing the transformation of those dry fields into a vision of beauty was that much more spectacular. I was able to capture a few photos to preserve that incredible sight.

CHAPTER 61

THE FORK IN THE ROAD

October 14, 2006—Age 10

Lukas had just finished a soccer game and he was with me as we were driving through the school parking lot. He looked up and saw a large beam of light coming through the clouds. He said, "I think that's a portal of light, and Jesus is the first to go up to heaven through it. Then all of the other people can follow him through the portal after they die."

Our last day in Marghita arrived and Iorela asked a question of Lukas and Gusztav that made my heart skip a beat. She said, "Do you want to drive out near the village where both of your birth mothers live?" Both boys answered, "Yes."

We got into the car and none of us spoke a word as we passed the sign with the name Marghita with a red slash through it, indicating that we were leaving that town. After we drove a few minutes farther, I noticed that we were in the midst of the sunflower fields that Sofia and I had visited to take photographs just the day before. My breathing was short and tight. I wondered what Lukas and Gusztav were feeling.

Iorela stopped the car at a fork in the road and we all got out of the car. She told them that their mothers' village was three miles down the road, along the fields of sunflowers. The boys posed for a photograph next to the sign that pointed to the town with a piercing depth in their eyes. Iorela and I waited for them to take the lead. Would they ask her to drive down that road toward the village, or would they turn around and return to Marghita? Without a word spoken, they both walked back into the car and then were silent. Iorela and I didn't need to ask. We sat quietly in the car as we drove, slowly losing sight of the fork in the road behind us. This was not the day or the time that they wanted to see that village or find their birth mothers. We were their mothers, and they were our sons.

The rest of the trip was amazing as well. We traveled to Sweden and visited with Jari and Carina and Henrika, Simon and Daniel. We picnicked and then swam in a beautiful lake, and shared memories from many years ago. They were volunteers I'd met in Romania, some of whom we hadn't seen in thirteen years. The trip was almost indescribable.

When we made our way back to San Diego and to our home, Lukas said to me, "I was rescued from that country. I could have grown up on the streets, living just like those children in that hut—poor, and without a chance in life—or like the teens without a family. I can't be a rinse and repeat kid." I asked him what he meant by a "rinse and repeat kid." He continued, "One that makes the same mistakes over and over again, rinse, repeat. I have to make something of my life. I cannot waste my life and waste being rescued. I think I have to come back here and help these people."

March 15, 2006—Age 10

Lukas was being teased by one boy in school about his difficulty with reading, spelling and school in general. The boy said that Lukas was so stupid, he shouldn't even bother coming to school. I asked Lukas what he felt God would think about the taunting comments. Lukas thought for a moment and then said, "There are rewards in heaven and you can lose them. I think if God would talk to him in heaven, He would say 'This is your reward in this box, but you called Lukas stupid, dumbo and bad at math. This was your reward, but you lost it. And the reward in this box was more than you could imagine.'" I had never talked to him about rewards in heaven, so I knew this was between him and God. After this, I think Lukas was less concerned about the terrible comments, and more about the consequences of teasing others. I hoped that this has served as a lesson to him about how to treat others.

That night, I walked into Lukas' room like I do every night and hugged him as I said, "I love you, Luke," while he returned the words, "I love you, Mom." He waited and then said, "Thank you so much for taking me back to Romania."

Moments later, as I sat in my room, I thought to myself, "Maybe the story isn't finished yet."

July 25, 2007—Age 11

Lukas and I were in the car and he said he was having another image from God. I had to pull over to write it down. Luckily I had paper in the car. He said, "At the end of the world, the souls go to heaven. The devil is in the center of the earth. The devil will unleash his power. He is angry that he's going to die and that he lost. His anger will destroy the earth. He creates the pit of fire at the center of the earth. Bad souls go into his chamber, like his prison." He thought for a minute and he said, "Why did He chose me to talk to people about this? I was born in Romania, born in a hut and lived in an orphanage, came from nothing, and had nothing. He could have chosen a millionaire and people would think that his words came from him alone. But he chose me. Maybe that's because he chooses the weak and poor to be the strong and wise."

He then said, "If we write the book with these things in them, the money doesn't belong to us. The money belongs to the suffering children." I had been thinking about the book that I thought I was to write, and I told him this sounded like a perfect idea.

PART III

KRISTI WILKINSON

EPILOGUE

Perhaps this should have been written as a forward, but I wanted to save some details until the end of the book. I wanted to share the impetus that finally prompted me to finish writing. My friend Stephanie Cain from Colorado—who had written to me while I lived in Romania, and who prayed for Lukas' adoption to come to fruition—was quite bold when she told me that I had to fulfill my dream to write the book. She said that it wasn't a choice, but a command from Lukas, and I had to finish it. I was struggling to find the time, as I worked full-time and also home-schooled my son because of his dyslexia and subsequent learning difficulties; finding down time where I felt the energy to write was almost impossible. One summer after finishing eighth grade, my son went with his friend's family on a week-long trip—the longest he had ever been away from home. I promised myself that I would commit that week to writing. I finished the first forty pages that week.

Several years passed as Lukas went through high school, and I just felt paralyzed by exhaustion and couldn't sit down at the computer. Homework with Lukas in the evenings after he finished classes and I finished work took us two to four hours every night. Needless to say, I had moved, and my computer was stored in my garage along with the book. January arrived, and so did that prompting, when the pastor of my church, Doug Kyle, gave a sermon on the "calling" that resides within. He asked everyone to respond to that one thing that they knew they needed to do. Perhaps it was a disguised New Year's resolution of sorts, but he suggested that it was more meaningful than that, and if possible, not to procrastinate, but to go out and do that "thing"—that deep desire, or to answer that "calling" that God had instilled in our hearts.

I knew immediately what that desire was for me. God had been nudging me to write for fourteen years, ever since I met with Doug and told him that I felt I had a story to tell. I knew what I needed to do. The next day, I went into the garage and I dug my dust-covered computer out of the recesses. I called a tech-wizard, Chris, who I had met at work, and I asked him to help me with my computer. He helped me to transfer what I had already written to another computer that was connected to the Internet. Need I mention that I am tech-challenged? I even wrote the first few pages of the book on paper, before transferring them to the screen. This was one of my stumbling blocks all along. But I was resolved not to allow my ill-feelings for technology to dissuade me from writing. Several weeks passed and I still couldn't sit down to write. That was until one Wednesday on a damp February morning.

I had started work at a rehab facility just a month prior—a big job change for me after eight years at a neighboring rehab facility. A patient named Burt, who had been in the building for a month, was on my treatment list for the first time. He had always been assigned to my co-worker, Marie, but she was taking the day off from work. I met Burt, and he was so energetic and had such a magnetic personality, we delved into conversation right away. We walked in the halls and exercised in the gym, and stopped off in his room to get a jacket before going outside to practice curbs and ramps with his walker. When in his room, I noticed a picture of his grandkids, and this led him to ask me if I had any kids. I don't usually mention that my son is adopted, but for some reason I mentioned this. Burt then said, "Where is your son from?" I told him that I adopted Lukas from Romania, and he responded with more fervor than expected, "Romania! I support a woman in Romania who works with the orphans and I have supported her for years. Maybe you know her."

Well, I mused, that would be rather unlikely—there were hundreds of volunteers there. Plus, I had worked in a tiny village that wasn't even on the map, and didn't work with any American volunteers while I was living there. So, I flippantly said, "Where did she do her work?" mostly expecting that it would be in a city far away from Lukas' birthplace. He replied, "The big city." To this I asked, "Bucharest?" He said, "I don't know, the big city,"

KRISTI WILKINSON

confirming my thoughts that I hadn't met her, as it was twelve hours away from Lukas' small village.

I thought I would throw him a bone, and so I said, "Burt, do you go to church in the area?" He said, "Yeah, I go to Maranatha." At that moment the hairs stood up on my arms and I asked, "Was her name Nann Gonzalez?" He excitedly said, "Yes, it is Nann. She is the one who I have supported all these years!"

I couldn't believe it. I did know Nann, more than just casually. So I said, "Burt, Nann housed Lukas and me in Bucharest for a few days when we were finalizing Lukas' adoption." She has also been to my house in San Diego as she brought an orphan to the states for a much needed surgery." He was as amazed as I was. So we headed outside into that cold February air, and we walked past a rose garden and talked about Romania and the orphans I met. As we were crossing a road to return to the building, he stopped abruptly. He said, "If there is something undone that you still are supposed to do, you have to do it. You have to listen to what God is telling you to do. You have to do it!" His message to me translated, "I must write this book and I have to do it now!"

I thought that was enough. I got the message. First Doug's sermon at the New Year, and now Burt. It was as if I was being told not waste another day. That next day, I worked with Burt on his final day before going home and we shared insights and excitement about Romania and I shared with him my dream about the book. He told me I should get in touch with Nann. I told him I didn't know how, that I hadn't gotten her newsletter in years and hadn't seen her in more than a decade. So I said my goodbyes and told him I wished him the best at home.

Within an hour, several people passed me as I was sitting at the nurses' station reviewing charts. First, a therapist named Michael came up to me and said, "Burt needs to talk to you. He really wants you to come to his room." "Hmm," I thought to myself, "I guess he just wants to talk about his return home." Next, another therapist named Amanda came up to me and repeated, "Burt says he needs to talk to you." I affirmed that I would go back. After a third therapist, Deborah, came up to me and said, "Burt wants you to come to his room," I figured I better leave my documentation and find Burt.

A few steps into his room, I noticed that he had a few visitors, and a few steps farther I noticed that an oxygen mask was strapped to his head to administer a breathing treatment. He ripped his oxygen mask off, and said, "You are not going to believe it. You are not going to believe it." I thought that his brother was going to wonder just who this crazy girl was who took priority over the oxygen treatment. He said, "I got a letter from Nann Gonzalez. I hadn't heard from her for a while, but my brother brought my mail, and she sent me a letter. It has her new phone number and address on it and you have to call her. You have to get in touch with her."

I was stunned. More than ten years had passed. Now my patient, Burt—whom I met because his scheduled therapist, Marie, needed to go to her son's sports event—had the number where I could reach Nann, whom I thought still lived in Romania. I thanked him immensely, and told him I just couldn't believe that he received that letter, the day before he went home. But then again I deeply believed it. I knew it was for me. I left the room and was overwhelmed with tears in my eyes.

A nurse in the hall named Aera said, "Kristi, are you OK?" I said, "It's a long story. I am fine. I am not sad, I am just amazed from something Burt gave to me." I explained just a short version of the story and told her that now I knew I needed to finish writing. I got into my car and called Nann, who now lived in Riverside, California. We talked and agreed that we should get together now that she lived stateside again.

Now, I thought that was it, however, that Saturday, I returned to an old workplace that I hadn't been to for several months to treat two patients. Before my day even started, I looked up from the nurse's station to see the name of a previous patient I had treated several times named Elizabeth. She was not one of the patients I was supposed to treat, but I really had a close bond with her after treating her several times, so I wanted to say hello. I walked into her room and was met by her son, Chuck. Now something hit me. There was something about her son, and I couldn't put my finger on it, but I remember long talks with Elizabeth about her son. Then a thought came to me. I said to him, "Were you a volunteer overseas?" He said, "Yes, I did work overseas." So I asked, "Where did you do the work?" as something inside me knew I had a connection to him. He said, "Romania." I

209

said, "That was it! Your mom and I would talk about your work with the orphans in Romania as I did work there with the children as well."

We then started talking about a book that he thought I would like about a man from Orange County, CA, who had left everything to live in Romania and help the people. This led to conversation about the book I wanted to write. He said that he would pray for me to get started. Then his daughter, Carolyn Hinkley—who had been listening to the conversation—said, "I am a writer and if you write the book, I could edit it for you." I was in awe. Just several days after meeting Burt, I was meeting another family that was motivating me to not only write the book, but that would edit the book for me. I found an editor before I was finished writing. I was on cloud nine. I got their numbers and told them that they would be hearing from me.

I was inspired and I knew what I needed to do. My excitement was palpable and I felt my heart racing along with a fire inside to finish what I had started. I went to church the next day and after the service, I almost couldn't wait to tell my pastor about the things that were unfolding. But there was one more thing. A woman named Michelle, who we had met in church, was dedicating her baby. My mom felt compelled to congratulate her family as she had seen the baby while sitting in back of us for the past few weeks. So I went up to talk to them as well.

My mom asked the grandmother of the child what the baby would call her. After hearing the response, my mom said, "My grandson calls me Nika, which is short for Bunica, the Romanian name for grandma." Michelle said, "Romania. I worked in Romania." I thought to myself, "Enough already. I get it." But then I asked, "Where did you work?" She said, "I was working with the orphans in Bucharest." Before she could say another word, I asked, "Did you work with Nann Gonzalez?" She responded, questioning, "Yes, How did you know? She is one of my best friends. I worked with her in Bucharest for ten years." I told her a short version of the story—leaving Burt out of it for the time being—but told her that Nann had housed Lukas, my mom, and me during the finalization of his adoption. She couldn't believe I knew Nann. I couldn't believe I was meeting the third person in one week that was related to Romania and the orphans there.

Immediately, I went out into the lobby and found my pastor, Doug Kyle, and I told him what had happened that week. I said that I had hooked up my computer, and that I would start to write again. I also mentioned that I didn't know what else God had planned, but I hoped it involved Nann Gonzalez. He was certainly making no mistake about that. The message was clear.

A few days later, after carving time away in the evenings after reading novels to my son for English class, I started writing. I wrote at every moment I found, and finished writing the book that May. I sent the rough draft to Carolyn Hinkley, and she stayed true to her word and edited it for me not only once, but twice. If that wasn't already an overwhelming act of kindness, she sent me an email, and let me know that before she even finished, she made a donation to an orphanage overseas in Lukas' honor. I couldn't believe it. God provided the momentum I needed to complete the "calling" that had been placed in me since the day I adopted ago, and she was fulfilling that calling, by making the first contribution to the children in need. Wasn't that what had prompted Lukas at age eleven to tell me it was time to write the story that God had spoken to his heart? The story that would someday help the children he left behind.

In the Fall of 2015, the book was undergoing its second edit and I decided to go on a woman's weekend at Palomar mountain with women from my church and any others that had interest. I had been going to my church for fifteen years, so I decided to make it a point to meet new people. On the first morning at breakfast, in a big cafeteria, I sat next to a girl I had never met named Deeanna Steffen. I found out that she was a single mom, and as I had been a single mom for eight years, we found it easy to find topics to share—everything from the horrors of dating to parenting. She asked about my son and before long I was sharing some of his adoption story. I told her about the amazing things unfolding to help me with the process of writing and editing the book. She told me that she would love to read it when I was finished, as did another woman I just met in my bunk room, and who was also eating breakfast with us, named Dawn Golding.

After breakfast, Dawn and I walked toward a multi-purpose room where a short message was to be shared before some of us headed out for a hike or horseback riding. Just before Dawn and I were ready to sit down, I spotted Deeanna sitting by herself in the back row of the room, so I said to Dawn, "Let's go over there and sit with Deeanna." Several seconds before I inched my way across the row to sit down, a woman I had never seen beat me to it and asked if she could sit next to Deeanna. So I scooted in front of both of them and took a seat next to the girl I still had yet not met. Dawn sat next to me on my left. As the still "unknown" girl was sitting next to me, I leaned past her and asked Deeanna if I could get her number. After the evening talk, I was planning on leaving the mountain and would not be spending the night like the rest of the women. I was keeping a list of everyone that expressed an interest in reading my book. I was planning on calling or emailing each one of them once it was published. But publishing it was the giant hurdle in front of me. I knew I could self-publish. My dad had done that for a book he wrote about teaching. I had talked to other writers about how to attempt publishing. Other people made it clear to me that finding a publisher as a new writer was quite a long-shot, or in other words, close to impossible.

When I leaned over, I said to Deeanna, "Can I get your number so I can call you when I finish my book?" The "unknown" girl must have been curious and she asked, "What book?"

I responded hesitantly, "Oh, it's a long story. It's about my son's adoption."

Her expression took on excitement and her eyes lit up. She said, "Tell me a little more about it."

I replied, "It really is a story about how I was able to adopt my son from Romania. I couldn't have coordinated all of the miracles if I tried." She then said, "Is it published yet?"

With a look of dismissal, I quipped, "Oh, no! I will probably just self-publish and have friends and family read it." (along with the others on the list I had kept in my special book).

She then answered with even more excitement, "I am a writer and I may be able to help you publish your book. I work for a publishing company and I would love to take a look at it if that is okay."

"Okay," I thought to myself. I could hardly believe it. I hadn't even finished the second edit, and I was meeting someone that might help me publish the book. The speaker was about ready to get started, so I jotted down the numbers of Deeanna, Dawn, and this new friend, named Beth Lottig, who was about to take the next step of the book writing process with me. I told her I just had to share more with her about the story before the weekend ended. My heart was racing.

Beth and I met at dinner later that day before I headed home. I shared a little more about Lukas and the thoughts and insights that he had as a young child. With emotion welling up in her eyes, she said to me, "Maybe this book isn't meant for just your family and friends. Maybe it is meant for more than that."

Beth continued to walk through the book publishing process with me. She encouraged me to make stylistic changes so that Lukas' thoughts would be woven throughout the story. Then she added a new assignment. She said, "Now it's time to make your book cover." I thought to myself, "Do I really have to create the book cover?" The simple thought of designing a book cover sent shivers down my spine. As far back as third grade, I had always been comfortable writing essays in class, but when a teacher required that the report needed a cover page with artistic flair, a wave of anxiety would sweep over me. I had the hardest time thinking of something creative, and to do this task on the computer could take me years. I had never uploaded a picture onto my computer or scanned images, let alone designed a book cover that might include photos. Somehow, I assumed that a publishing company would want to design their own cover for my book, so I had not anticipated this new task.

Since I was not inherently born with a gift for graphics—especially in design—I had already asked my friend from high school, Sharon Okamoto, to help me with choices for the font and chapter headings. She was a graphic designer by trade as well as a talented artist, so I knew she could give me some ideas. We had spent hours in her home as teenagers making renderings in charcoal and pencil for art class, and she had continued to use her skills in this area for decades. But a thought came to me— maybe I could ask her to help me with the design of the book cover.

I called Sharon and asked her if she might be able to help me with ideas for the cover. She immediately responded, "I do book covers for a living. Of course I could help you with this." Being more than humble about her career, I knew these covers included those she was commissioned to do for special book editions for Time Magazine. It hit me then. Sharon, the former assistant art director for Time Magazine, would be designing my book cover. I couldn't even have dreamed of this! She responded, "I will have time to help you with this right after I finish the special edition issue for Gene Wilder." He had just passed away and she had been commissioned by Time for this project. I was extremely humbled and almost speechless that my cover design would be the next that she would do after his.

She then asked, "What is your sub-head?" I asked her, "What do you mean by sub-head?" She explained that it was a sub-heading, or quick synopsis of the story, said as succinctly as possible, to give the reader an idea of what the book was about. It would also be on the cover of the book. Since I didn't even know what one was, I was relieved that she was informing me of the necessary details to be included in a book cover. Next, she asked me to talk to Lukas, as she knew he had an artistic mind, to see if he had an idea for the cover photograph that she would use. Lukas immediately had an image come to mind. He wanted the image to include him as a toddler walking away from his orphanage. Not a single photograph that fit this description surfaced from a sea of over 700 photos that I had taken. Sharon then told me to send her some photos that Lukas and I thought might work, and she called me and said, "One of the pictures will be perfect." It was the same image that I had in mind. It was a photograph of Lukas that I had taken of him at age ten. This was also the same age many of his insights had come to him—insights that made it onto the pages of my journal. Somehow, this picture seemed fitting, as he had a contemplative expression that captured his spirit and also matched the title he had chosen at about that age, The Child Who Listens. I hoped that his expression would speak to someone's heart. Within weeks, she sent seven cover designs from which to choose. I was now on my way to the finishing touches of the book.

I am not sure how many people will have an interest in reading this book that I felt "called" to write and this story Lukas told me I must tell. I hope it touches at least one heart. I am not sure what the future will hold. But I pray that it involves Lars, Nann, and the fatherless children in Romania.

February 25, 2004—Age 8

Lukas and I were on a walk and the wind was blowing, the clouds were shifting, and the sun was setting with many colors in the sky as we made our way up a hill toward our house. He then said to me, "Do you know what God is showing me?" I answered, "No I don't. Tell me what you see." He went on to say, "Jesus sewed us into a quilt. He sewed us into our own quilt. It's like we're part of a quilt that he stitched together. We have our own patterns and designs that He gave to us. He wants to sew us all together. People from everywhere in the world. When you sew it all together, you see the humongous quilt of the world that He made. We only get to see part of the whole quilt when we're here. But when we die, if we believe in God, then we get taken off the quilt and we go to heaven and we're able to see the whole quilt from every side. When we die, it's like we're set free to see it the way He made it, all the way around. But we have to wait until we get to heaven to see the whole quilt." I was struck with his vision of what part we played in the world's picture and what it might be like someday after we leave this place we call home.

The End

MORE THOUGHTS
FROM LUKAS

Although the next several entries are not spiritual in nature, I wanted to include them to reflect his personality.

July 2000—Age 4

Lukas was about to have x-rays prior to surgery to remove very swollen adenoids. We had been reading about Curious George's trips to the hospital to prepare him for the tests. As we sat in the waiting room, he looked around with a puzzled expression in his face and asked, "Mama, where are all the monkeys?" Even though this didn't have a deep spiritual lesson, it showed me how kids viewed their surroundings in a completely literal way.

September 11, 2002—Age 6

Lukas and I were shopping, and he asked me what we were going to get Jesus for his birthday. He answered his own question by saying, "We have to write him a note, and tie it to a balloon and send it to heaven." I was sure that we would tie a note onto a balloon and release it heavenward on Christmas day.

June 24, 2003—Age 7

Lukas asked me one day, "Mom, how do you turn the world upside down?" I asked, "How?" He replied, "Stand on your head."

May 8, 2003—Age 7

Lukas was developing a blister on his toe from his sneakers and he insisted he didn't want to get new shoes. I tried to convince him he needed new shoes and I said, "It's dangerous not to get new shoes." He replied emphatically, "It's not dangerous, Mom. Dropping off a 2,000-foot cliff without a parachute—that's dangerous." He always was quick to see the truth of the matter.

August 4, 2005—Age 9

We were reading *The Cat and the Hat* by Dr. Seuss, and we were looking at a page with Thing One running down a long hallway. Lukas said, "I think sometimes Dr. Seuss forgets his outside perimeter, because at the beginning of the book, the house looks so small." I wouldn't change a thing about Dr. Seuss' illustrations, but I chuckled at his observation.

February 14, 2016—Age 20

Lukas went to church at Green Valley with my family and listened to the sermon given by a guest pastor in his seventies, as Doug Kyle, our lead pastor, was out of town for the week. This seasoned speaker named David Sunde discussed relationships, a fitting topic for Valentine's Day. After he spoke, Lukas said, "Listening to that pastor made me think. He was an older man, and he was so wise and intelligent. If only we could live with the wisdom of an older man. If we had that passion and wisdom in us at our young age, how much different our lives would be. But as they say, 'wisdom comes with experience which comes with age.'"

WORKS CITED

Groza, Victor, Ileana, Daniela, Irwin, Ivor. *A Peacock or a Crow: Stories, Interviews and Commentaries on Romanian Adoptions.* Toronto: Lakeshore Communications, 1999. Print.

Kristi holding Lukas on Christmas Eve, shortly
after meeting him at Casa Alba

A commonplace sight on the streets of Marghita

Kristi with teenagers from the orphanage in Cadea, Lukas far left

Iorela with Gusztav at Casa Alba

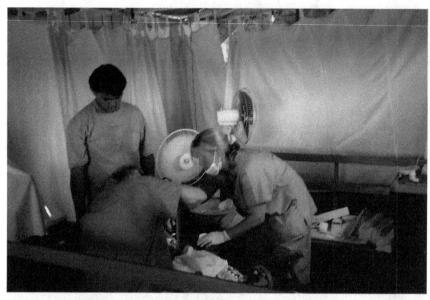

Kristi assisting a dentist at a medical clinic on the Amazon River

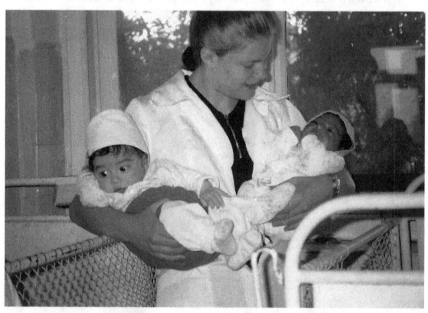

Courtney Brown at age 16, holding babies orphaned
at the hospital (Lukas in her right arm)

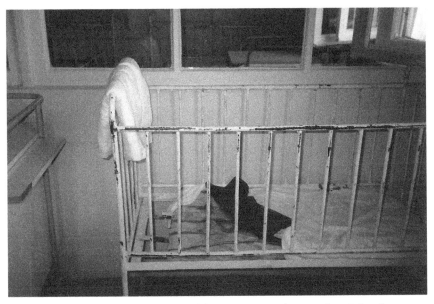

Crib for an orphan with moldy mattress in hospital in Marghita

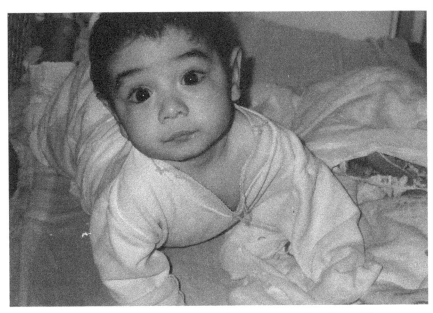

Lukas at the hospital prior to being chosen for Casa Alba

Courtney Brown and Kristi's mom, Sandi,
holding orphans at the hospital

Kristi at Casa Alba with Lukas on left, Gusztav on right

Merchant at the marketplace in Marghita (summertime)

Kristi getting her hair cut by a Cadea teen in training
by Phyllis (in background wearing white T-shirt)

Kristi baking cookies with teens from Cadea

Toddlers Kristi cared for at Casa Alba

Lukas' birth mother with his half-siblings in
front of his first home, a straw hut

Kristi's reunion with Lukas, Iorela, and Guzstav at
the Oradea Airport, weeks before his adoption

Kristi and Sandi Wilkinson at Lukas' goodbye
party the day before he left the orphanage

Lukas, Kristi, and Sandi in the cockpit of the
plane en route to America, May 2000

Homecoming at the San Diego Airport, on day of arrival
in U.S. From far left, Kristi, sister Julie Peccedi, Lukas, Jim
Wilkinson, Katie and Laurie Leasure, Carolyn Hess.

Lukas, age four, weeks after his move to Denver, CO

Kristi, Lukas, Gusztav, and Iorela at a reunion in La Jolla, CA, in 2003

Gusztav and Lukas during reunion in Point Loma, CA

Lukas on return to his orphanage, Casa Alba, age 17

Kristi and Lukas in Casa Alba, 2013

Gusztav and Lukas on playground at Casa
Alba during reunion trip in 2013

Lukas with his sister, Silvia, in Marghita (first
time he had seen her in 13 years)

Iorela, Kristi, Henrika, and Carina, reunited in
Mariestad, Sweden (all volunteers in Romania)

The toddlers Kristi cared for from the "Yellow Room"
(from left, Gusztav, Lukas, Csaba, Otto)

Kristi shopping for fruit at the market in China

Beds the teens slept on at the orphanage at Cadea

Lukas and his roommate, Laurentiu, walk hand
in hand on the streets of Marghita

Evening meal with volunteers at Herculane, the volunteer house in
Marghita (Barbro seated far left, and Lars Gustavsson far right)

ABOUT THE AUTHOR

Kristi Wilkinson spent her youth in Pennsylvania, and has served as a physical therapist, youth leader, foster parent, and community volunteer. She earned a Bachelor of Arts from University of Richmond in 1989, and a Master of Physical Therapy from Hahnemann University in Philadelphia in 1991. She has practiced for ten years as a physical therapist for a geriatric population and for brain injured adults in Denver, Colorado. Kristi has worked as a physical therapist for a geriatric population in San Diego for seventeen years. She has served as a youth counselor for five years in Denver, Colorado, volunteered with the homeless in San Diego, and currently serves as a mentor for foster youth in San Diego. She has traveled internationally as a volunteer therapist to Kazakhstan, China, Brazil, and Romania, ultimately adopting her son from Romania.

Proceeds from this book will be given to support orphans around the globe. To further assist the children of Romania, donations can also be made to Father's Care Ministry, Inc. using the contact information below.

2118 Cedar St.
Bakersfield, CA 93301
email: fcm.worldwide@gmail.com
phone: 661-900-3833.

Please include "The Child Who Listens" in subject line if making a donation.